Lecture Notes in Computer Science

Lecture Notes in Artificial Intelligence **14917**

Founding Editor

Jörg Siekmann

The series Lecture Notes in Artificial Intelligence (LNAI) was established in 1988 as a topical subseries of LNCS devoted to artificial intelligence.

The series publishes state-of-the-art research results at a high level. As with the LNCS mother series, the mission of the series is to serve the international R & D community by providing an invaluable service, mainly focused on the publication of conference and workshop proceedings and postproceedings.

Wenpeng Yin · Jihyun Janice Ahn · Rui Zhang ·
Lifu Huang · Rafik Hadfi · Takayuki Ito ·
Susumu Ohnuma · Shun Shiramatsu
Editors

Artificial Intelligence for Research and Democracy

First International Workshop, AI4Research 2024
and 4th International Workshop, DemocrAI 2024
Held in Conjunction with IJCAI 2024
Jeju, South Korea, August 5, 2024
Proceedings

Springer

Editors
Wenpeng Yin
Pennsylvania State University
Pennsylvania, PA, USA

Jihyun Janice Ahn
Pennsylvania State University
Pennsylvania, PA, USA

Rui Zhang
Pennsylvania State University
Pennsylvania, PA, USA

Lifu Huang
University of California, Davis
California, CA, USA

Rafik Hadfi
Kyoto University
Kyoto, Kyoto, Japan

Takayuki Ito
Kyoto University
Kyoto, Kyoto, Japan

Susumu Ohnuma
Hokkaido University
Sapporo, Hokkaido, Japan

Shun Shiramatsu
Nagoya Institute of Technology
Nagoya, Aichi, Japan

ISSN 0302-9743 ISSN 1611-3349 (electronic)
Lecture Notes in Artificial Intelligence
ISBN 978-981-97-9535-2 ISBN 978-981-97-9536-9 (eBook)
https://doi.org/10.1007/978-981-97-9536-9

LNCS Sublibrary: SL7 – Artificial Intelligence

This Springer imprint is published by the registered company Springer Nature Singapore Pte Ltd.
The registered company address is: 152 Beach Road, #21-01/04 Gateway East, Singapore 189721, Singapore

Preface of AI4Research Workshop

As the Organizing Chair, I am pleased to welcome readers to the proceedings of AI4Research 2024, a workshop co-located with IJCAI 2024—The 33rd International Joint Conference on Artificial Intelligence. IJCAI 2024 was held in Jeju, South Korea, from August 3–9, 2024, as an in-person event. The conference served as an interdisciplinary platform to explore how recent AI advancements are influencing scientific research across various fields. Discussions ranged from ethical considerations arising from the capabilities of modern large language models to technical challenges and solutions for the responsible use of AI in supporting and accelerating research. The AI4Research 2024 program featured three keynote talks and five oral presentations of accepted papers.

Keynotes:

AI as A Tool, AI as A Master and Some Ethics in Between
By Marija Slavkovik, University of Bergen, Norway

AI-Accelerated Discovery through Dataset Augmentation
By Zachary G. Ives, University of Pennsylvania, USA

Learning Foundation Language Models for Geoscience Knowledge Understanding and Utilization
By Zhouhan Lin, Shanghai Jiao Tong University, China

Preface of DemocrAI 2024 Workshop

We are pleased to present the proceedings of the 4th International Workshop on Democracy and AI (DemocrAI 2024), held in conjunction with the International Joint Conference on Artificial Intelligence (IJCAI). This workshop explores the potential of AI-assisted democracy to overcome geographical, cultural, religious, and ethnic divides, promoting new forms of democratic decision-making.

The key topics of this year's workshop included democratic online platforms, formal theories of collective decision-making, and advanced methodologies for discourse analysis. This year, we received eleven submissions, each reviewed in a rigorous double-blind process by at least three reviewers. From these, five papers were selected for inclusion, representing innovative contributions to AI-assisted democracy.

We would like to express our appreciation to all contributors, organizers, and participants. We hope these proceedings will inspire further research and innovation in AI-assisted democracy, contributing to more inclusive and fair democratic processes.

June 2024

Rafik Hadfi
Takayuki Ito
Susumu Ohnuma
Shun Shiramatsu

AI4Research Workshop Organization

Organizing Chairs

Wenpeng Yin	Pennsylvania State University, USA
Jihyun Janice Ahn	Pennsylvania State University, USA
Rui Zhang	Pennsylvania State University, USA
Lifu Huang	University of California, Davis, USA

Advisory Board

Najoung Kim	Boston University, USA
Wei Xu	Georgia Institute of Technology, USA
Muhao Chen	University of California, Davis, USA
Heike Adel	Hochschule der Medien, Germany

Technical Program Committee

Yunxuan Li	Google, USA
Zhifei Zhang	Tongji University, China
Hongyu Li	Yale University, USA
Yuge Wang	Yale University, USA
Tianyu Liu	Yale University, USA
Qingyun Wang	University of Illinois at Urbana-Champaign, USA
Huan Ning	Pennsylvania State University, USA
Yixiang Yao	University of Southern California, USA
Berk Atıl	Pennsylvania State University, USA
Wenjie Jacky Mo	University of California, Davis, USA
Jiangshu Du	University of Illinois at Chicago, USA
A. M. Muntasir Rahman	New Jersey Institute of Technology, USA
Junyi Ye	New Jersey Institute of Technology, USA
Di Liu	Temple University, USA
Ibraheem Muhammad Moosa	Pennsylvania State University, USA
Hanzi Xu	Temple University, USA
Zhaohui Li	State University of New York at Buffalo, USA
Renze Lou	Pennsylvania State University, USA
Sarkar Snigdha Sarathi Das	Pennsylvania State University, USA

Nan Zhang	Pennsylvania State University, USA
Quan Li	Pennsylvania State University, USA
Amutheezan Sivagnanam	Pennsylvania State University, USA
Jiazhao Li	University of Michigan, USA
Jiangtao Liu	Pennsylvania State University, USA
Xin Dong	TikTok, USA
Xiaozhi Zhu	University of Notre Dame, USA
Sixing Chen	University of Pennsylvania, USA
Yusen Zhang	Pennsylvania State University, USA

DemocrAI 2024 Workshop Organization

Organizing Committee

Rafik Hadfi	Kyoto University, Japan
Takayuki Ito	Kyoto University, Japan
Susumu Ohnuma	Hokkaido University, Japan
Shun Shiramatsu	Nagoya Institute of Technology, Japan

Program Committee Chairs

Carlos Rodrigo Garibay Rubio	Kyoto University, Japan
Jawad Ahmad Haqbeen	Kyoto University, Japan
Kyung Ryul Park	Korea Advanced Institute of Science and Technology, South Korea
Naoki Fukuta	Shizuoka University, Japan
Nobutsugu Kanzaki	Nanzan University, Japan
Shigeo Matsubara	Osaka University, Japan
Shiyao Ding	Kyoto University, Japan
Shun Okuhara	Nagoya Institute of Technology, Japan
Takanobu Otsuka	Nagoya Institute of Technology, Japan
Tessai Hayama	Nagaoka University of Technology, Japan
Tokuro Matsuo	Advanced Institute of Industrial Technology, Japan
Victoria Huang	National Institute of Water and Atmospheric Research, New Zealand
Weihua Li	Auckland University of Technology, New Zealand

Contents

Poster

AI for Research

Educational Research Trends of the Use of Gaze Learning Data Through Topic Modeling and Scientometric Analysis

Jungmin Lee[1], Huigon Shin[2], YoungJoon Yoo[3], Jongwon Choi[1,3], and Mi Song Kim[4(✉)]

[1] Department of Advanced Imaging, GSAIM, Chung-Ang University, Seoul, Republic of Korea
[2] Computer Programming and Analysis, School of Information Technology, Fanshawe College, London, Canada
[3] Department of Artificial Intelligence, Chung-Ang University, Seoul, Republic of Korea
[4] Curriculum Studies, Western University, London, Canada
mkim574@uwo.ca

Abstract. Multimodal learning analytics have become increasingly important in enabling a deeper understanding of teaching and learning in educational research. However, in comparison to other multimodal learning data, there is a limited understanding of the trends within gaze learning data. To address this challenge, this study aims to identify latent topics in gaze learning data through topic modeling and scientometric analysis. We analyzed the abstracts of 573 peer-reviewed and conference proceeding papers that used gaze learning data, written in English, and published between 2008 and February 2024. The findings are as follows. First, three main topics were identified through topic modeling analysis: (learning analytics, multimodal learning, and inclusive learning). Second, the scientometric analysis revealed the structure in which diverse clusters in cited references and institutions are connected around the emerging topics. Based on these findings, the study would provide insights into research directions in both educational research and applications using gaze learning data.

Keywords: Topic Modeling · Scientometric Analysis · Educational Research

1 Introduction

In alignment with an increasingly acknowledged emphasis on digital technology generating a vast amount of multimodal learning data within educational research, the utilization of learners' multimodal data is integral to the development and implementation of innovative pedagogical and curriculum strategies [8]. Specifically, collaboration learning has been promoted by utilizing digital technologies such as game-based learning, mobile learning, and simulations.

J. Lee and H. Shin—These authors contributed equally to this work.

W. Yin et al. (Eds.): IJCAI 2024, LNAI 14917, pp. 3–19, 2025.
https://doi.org/10.1007/978-981-97-9536-9_1

Just placing individual learners in a group does not inherently signify evidence of collaborative learning facilitated through these technologies.

Growing interests has emerged regarding the integration of gaze behavior patterns to enhance idea improvements in collaborative learning. There is great evidence of successful interactions by the coordination of attention and gaze across a shared visual space [2]. However, other multimodal learning data, gaze-based educational research is still in its early stages.

To address this challenge, this study aims to explore what are the main educational research trends of the use of gaze learning data through topic modeling and scientometric analysis. Our overall analysis was shaped by two research questions: (1) What are the main topics of gaze in educational research through topic modeling approach developed by our research team and scientometric analysis? and (2) What are the implications of the research findings on topic modeling and scientometric analysis as presented in this study?

2 Theoretical Background

Educational research has indicated that multimodal learning data such as "linguistic, visual, audio, gestural, spatial and multimodal designs" [9], provide affordances, enabling embodied and more interactive opportunities for communication and meaning-making in fostering collaboration. Overall, the affordances of multimodal learning data empower both students and teachers to engage in more authentic and dynamic forms of learning across formal and informal contexts.

In this manner, gaze-based educational research also offers several benefits in understanding learning experiences and improving educational practices. These benefits of eye gaze data encompass (a) offering valuable insights into the level of learner engagement by tracking their visual attention towards targeted instructional materials or interventions, (b) tracking learners' specific learning process visually through monitoring their fixations and saccades, (c) identifying areas of difficulty or confusion employed by learners during learning tasks by measuring prolonged fixations and frequent regressions, and (d) enhancing learner interaction design and tools using technologies by examining user experience.

To quantitatively examine research trends in gaze educational research, we conducted a scientometric analysis emphasizing publication patterns, citation networks, and collaboration among educational researchers [14]. For such analysis, we adopt techniques such as topic modeling [1] and scientometric analysis to qualitatively and quantitatively illustrate the semantic shifts in educational papers related to gaze.

3 Document Analysis Using Topic Model

In this section, we encapsulate the core principles of the topic model, highlighting two prevalent approaches: (1) semantic topic extraction across entire documents and (2) document clustering based on the identified topics. With K topics denoted as $\beta_k \in \boldsymbol{\beta}, k = 1, ..., K$, the topic model allocates documents to one of these topics, constituting a clustering procedure based on the topics. This allocation can be deterministic or generative, achieved by specifying the topic distribution for each document as follows:

$$z_{dn} \sim p_{\theta_d}(z), \tag{1}$$

In the generative process, the distribution $p_{\theta_d}(z)$ selects the index variable z_{dn}, representing the topic index $\beta_{z_{dn}}$ encompassing the word w_{dn} within the d-th document. Typically, in a generative framework, the random variable $\boldsymbol{\theta}$ follows a K-dimensional Categorical distribution [1] with a Dirichlet prior α, or a Product of Expert (PoE) [16].

Each topic β_k is characterized by a set of semantically coherent words $w_{kn} \in \beta_k, 1, ..., N_w$, or alternatively, by a generatively defined word distribution, as follows:

$$w_k \sim p_{\beta_k}(w). \tag{2}$$

Similarly, $p_{\beta_k}(w)$ may adopt categorical-like distributions [1]. Classical probabilistic generative topic models [1,16] interpret each document d as a Bag-of-Words (BoW) $\mathbf{w}_d = w_{d1}, ..., w_{dn}$ and analyze the joint distribution $p(\boldsymbol{\theta}, \boldsymbol{\beta}|\mathbf{w}_d)$ from Eqs. (1–2), employing approximated Bayesian inference methods [3,10,17].

When embedding is integrated into topic modeling frameworks [6,13], certain branches of embedded topic models retain the word generation ability, thus incorporating word embedding into their probabilistic framework, as observed in ETM [6]. Non-generative embedded topic models, including recent PLM-based topic models [7,15], directly extract topic embedding via distance-based clustering methods, circumventing complex Bayesian inference approximations.

Table 1. A summary of search criteria and procedure for data collection.

Setting up search criteria	Database	Web of Science
Initial retrieval	Search String	Gaze * (learning or teaching or education or instruction)
Fine-tuning retrieval	Retrieved abstract	573 results
	Publication years	From 2008 to 2024
	Document types	Article, Proceeding paper
	Languages	English
	Research areas	Education educational research
Final retrieval	Retrieved full papers	463 results

Table 2. A network summary of cited references.

Indicators	Cited Reference
Time span (co-citation)	2014–2024
Nodes (cited references)	683
Edges (citations)	1,999
Density	0.0086
Modularity	0.9073
Mean Silhouette	0.9683

Fig. 1. Clusters for cited references.

4 Methodology

As illustrated in Table 1, the PRISMA procedure [12] was employed to identify relevant peer-reviewed or proceeding studies published in English since 2008, a period characterized by a substantial increase in scholarly output, particularly observed in the Web of Science database, renowned as one of the most popular databases in educational research. The process of selecting relevant educational studies on gaze was guided by keywords such as 'gaze' with 'learning' or 'teaching' or 'education' or 'instruction.'

4.1 Topic Modeling

To embark on topic extraction and evaluation, we commence by preprocessing the input documents in accordance with the established conventions outlined in [1]. Upon varying the number of topics, our initial endeavor involves qualitatively visualizing the dominant words within each topic. Furthermore, to undertake a quantitative assessment of topic quality, we proceed to evaluate the

Table 3. Cluster summary for cited references.

ID	Size	Silhouette	Mean	Top 5 Terms (LLR)
0	54	0.963	2019	Instructional settings Prompting Specific task instruction Mixed methods Preservice teacher education
1	48	0.943	2016	Multimedia learning Eye movement modeling examples Learning performance Teaching Eye gaze
2	41	0.974	2019	Learning performance Eye gaze Video lectures Facial expression Teacher research
9	22	1.000	2012	School Special education Social interaction Attention Teaching
12	17	0.978	2017	multimodality Mathematics Gesture Design Embodiment
14	17	0.990	2019	Teaching statistics Coordination dynamics Histogram Learning analytics Machine learning algorithm

model's efficacy concerning Topic Quality (TQ) and its ability to represent documents, in alignment with the standardized evaluation framework devised for topic models.

The evaluation of TQ hinges upon two pivotal metrics: Topic Coherence (TC) and Topic Diversity (TD). TC is appraised through the utilization of cross-validated (CV) coherence, a metric devised to gauge the semantic coherence exhibited by the principal words encapsulated within each topic. The CV-coherence scores span a spectrum from 0 to 1, with higher values indicative of enhanced interpretability and semantic coherence. On the other hand, TD serves as a measure of word diversity, quantified by calculating the unique count of words amongst the top 25 words across all topics [6]. TD scores range between 0 and 1, with elevated values signifying a more diverse array of words present.

4.2 Scientometric Analysis

An analysis software, CiteSpace version 6.3.R3 [4], was adopted to analyze and visualize the citation patterns and the network of clusters of co-cited publications. In the network, a node indicates a cited reference or institutions where the publications were released. Two nodes are connected by an edge, indicating an occurrence of a citation. The clusters of the co-cited publications were visualized and entitled based on the titles, keywords, and abstracts of the co-cited publications [5]. Two indicators, modularity and silhouette, demonstrate how the network is structured. Specifically, modularity denotes the level of loosely distinctive division of the network into clusters. Silhouette indicates the homogeneity of the clusters in the network on average [4]. Further, a citation burst is created founded on a burst-detection algorithm [11] "for detecting sharp increases of interest in a specialty," which is enabled and "identified based on such burst terms extracted from titles, abstracts, descriptors, and identifiers of bibliographic records" [5]. Thus, the publication with a burst is the emerging research with a spotlight in the field.

5 Findings

5.1 Scientometric Analysis

Cited Reference Analysis. Table 2 indicated the density and modularity of the identified 6 clusters out of 132 clusters in the network of the cited references. The network has high modularity (0.9073) and silhouette (0.9683) values, indicating the homogeneity of the clusters.

Figure 1 and Table 3 show the top six clusters identified through keyword analysis: "instructional settings" (54 references, the mean year of 2019, silhouette value of 0.963), "multimedia learning" (48 references, the mean year of 2016, silhouette value of 0.943), "learning performance" (41 references, the mean year of 2019, silhouette value of 0.974), "school" (22 references, the mean year of 2012, silhouette value of 1), "multimodality" (17 references, the mean year of 2017, silhouette value of 0.978), "teaching statistics" (17 references, the mean year of 2019, silhouette value of 0.99).

The examination of co-cited references revealed that publications have been increasingly cited over time. Figure 2 shows the top 8 publications that were discovered through the citation burst detection. Since 2016, these studies have been cited abruptly.

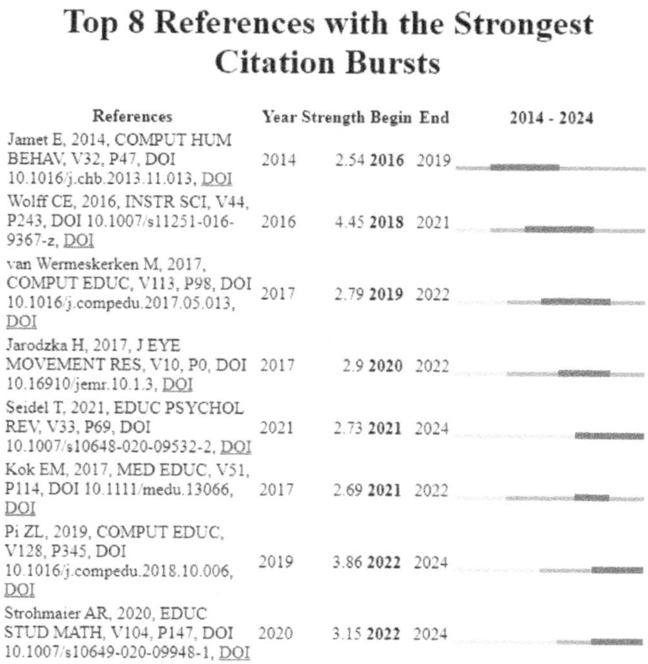

Top 8 References with the Strongest Citation Bursts

References	Year	Strength	Begin	End	2014 - 2024
Jamet E, 2014, COMPUT HUM BEHAV, V32, P47, DOI 10.1016/j.chb.2013.11.013, DOI	2014	2.54	**2016**	2019	
Wolff CE, 2016, INSTR SCI, V44, P243, DOI 10.1007/s11251-016-9367-z, DOI	2016	4.45	**2018**	2021	
van Wermeskerken M, 2017, COMPUT EDUC, V113, P98, DOI 10.1016/j.compedu.2017.05.013, DOI	2017	2.79	**2019**	2022	
Jarodzka H, 2017, J EYE MOVEMENT RES, V10, P0, DOI 10.16910/jemr.10.1.3, DOI	2017	2.9	**2020**	2022	
Seidel T, 2021, EDUC PSYCHOL REV, V33, P69, DOI 10.1007/s10648-020-09532-2, DOI	2021	2.73	**2021**	2024	
Kok EM, 2017, MED EDUC, V51, P114, DOI 10.1111/medu.13066, DOI	2017	2.69	**2021**	2022	
Pi ZL, 2019, COMPUT EDUC, V128, P345, DOI 10.1016/j.compedu.2018.10.006, DOI	2019	3.86	**2022**	2024	
Strohmaier AR, 2020, EDUC STUD MATH, V104, P147, DOI 10.1007/s10649-020-09948-1, DOI	2020	3.15	**2022**	2024	

Fig. 2. Burstness for cited references.

In Figs. 3 and 4, the timeline and time zone provide a representation of the progression of cited references over time, offering insights into the development of research themes. The timeline and time zone visualizations demonstrate the significant evolution of gaze-related research from 2014 to 2024.

Institution Analysis. Table 4 indicated the density and modularity of the identified 5 clusters out of 114 clusters in the network of the institutions. The network has high modularity (0.9073) and silhouette (0.9683) values the same as the network of cited references, indicating the homogeneity of the clusters.

Figure 5 and Table 5 show the top five clusters identified through keyword analysis: "multimodal data" (18 references, the mean year of 2018, silhouette value of 0.926), "facial expression" (13 references, the mean year of 2020, silhouette value of 0.948), "virtual reality" (9 references, the mean year of 2017, silhouette value of 1), "2-translanguaging" (7 references, the mean year of 2019, silhouette value of 0.993), "design exploration" (5 references, the mean year of 2018, silhouette value of 1).

The examination of co-institution revealed that a publication has been cited explosively. Figure 6 shows one publication from Central China Normal University that was discovered through citation burst detection. Since 2022, this study has been cited abruptly.

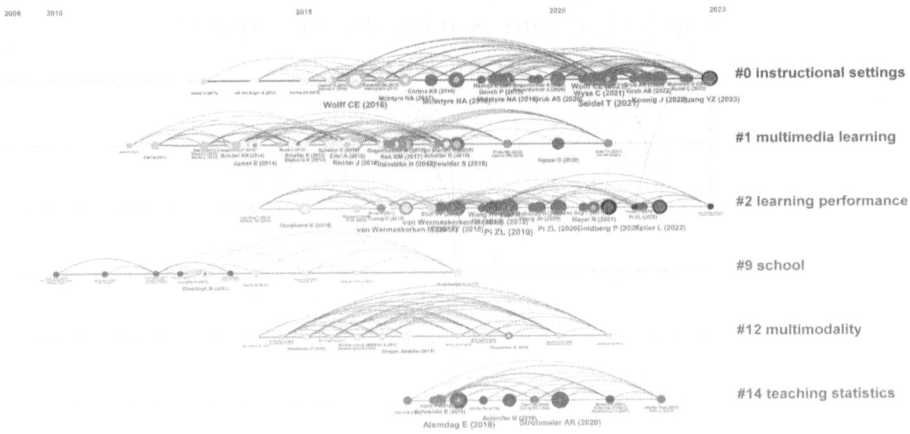

Fig. 3. Timeline for cited references.

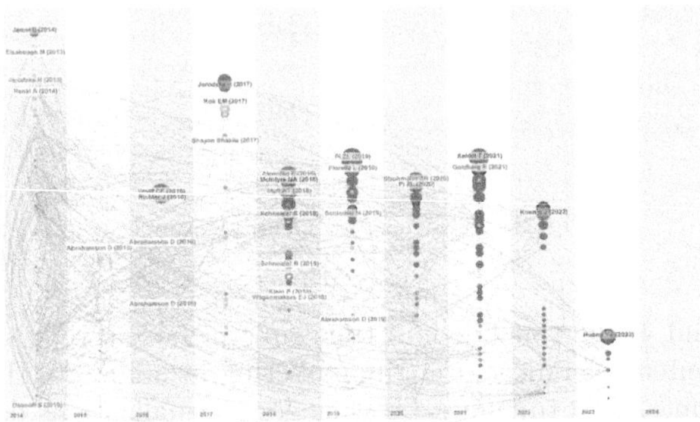

Fig. 4. Time zone for cited references.

In Figs. 7 and 8, like cited references, the timeline and time zone represent the progression of institution publications over time, offering insights into developing research themes. The timeline and time zone visualizations demonstrate the significant evolution of gaze-related research from 2014 to 2024.

5.2 Topic Modeling

Quantitative Evaluation. We examine the performance of algorithms for topic modeling using LDA [1] and BERTopic [7]. Increasing the number of topics from ten to fifty at ten-topic intervals, we evaluate TC and TD subsequently by computing the mean of these metrics. Results depicted in Fig. 9 reveal that LDA maintains a TC of 0.374, indicating the presence of semantically consistent topics to a certain extent. BERTopic, however, achieves a TC of 0.733, signaling a generation of topics with substantially greater consistency as compared to LDA.

Table 4. A network summary of institutions.

Indicators	Institution
Time span (co-citation)	2014–2024
Nodes (institutions)	238
Edges (citations)	221
Density	0.0075
Modularity	0.9073
Mean Silhouette	0.9683

Fig. 5. Clusters for institutions.

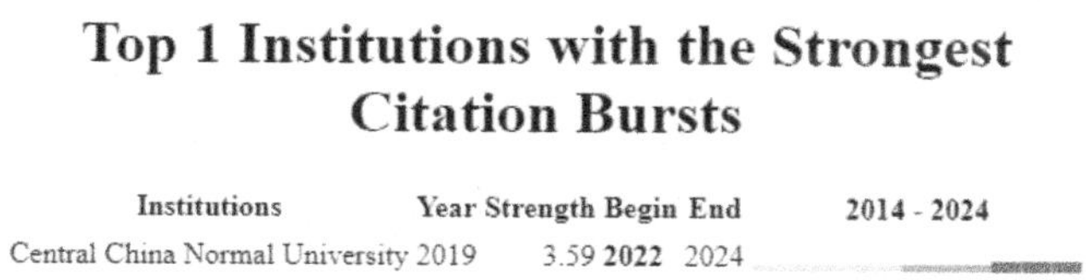

Fig. 6. Burstness for institutions.

TD also displays a stark contrast, with LDA registering a value of 0.185 against BERTopic of 0.9275, highlighting a significantly wider array of topics from the latter.

The visual representation in Fig. 10 contrasts TQ for both LDA and BERTopic across varying topic counts. BERTopic consistently surpasses LDA

Table 5. Cluster summary for institutions.

ID	Size	Silhouette	Mean	Top 5 Terms (LLR)
0	18	0.926	2018	Multimodal data Students' performance Tangible user interfaces Embodied learning Eye tracking
1	13	0.948	2020	Facial expression Instructor-generated outlines Teacher preparation Pedagogy Instructor presence
2	9	1.000	2017	Virtual reality Engagement Simulation Scholarship of teaching and learning Visual attention
6	7	0.993	2019	2-translanguaging 3-race Problem solving /decision making 1-early childhood Organic chemistry
9	5	1.000	2018	Design exploration Educational technology Vocational education and training Vet Its

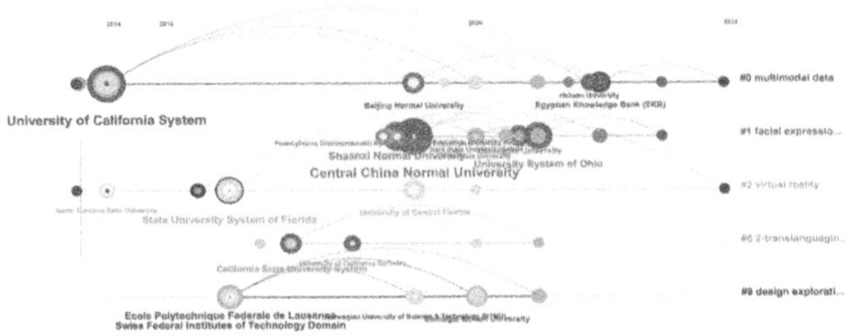

Fig. 7. Timeline for institutions.

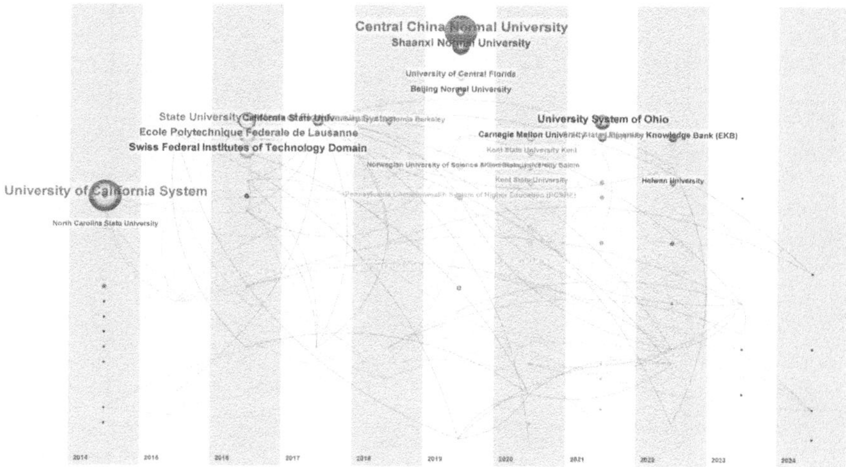

Fig. 8. Time zone for institutions.

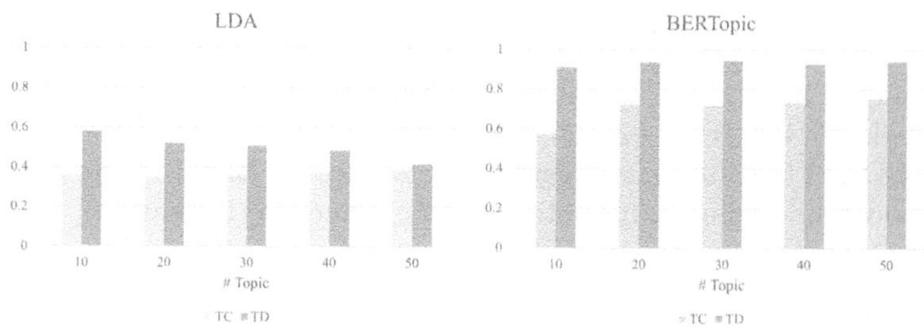

Fig. 9. Comparison of TC and TD.

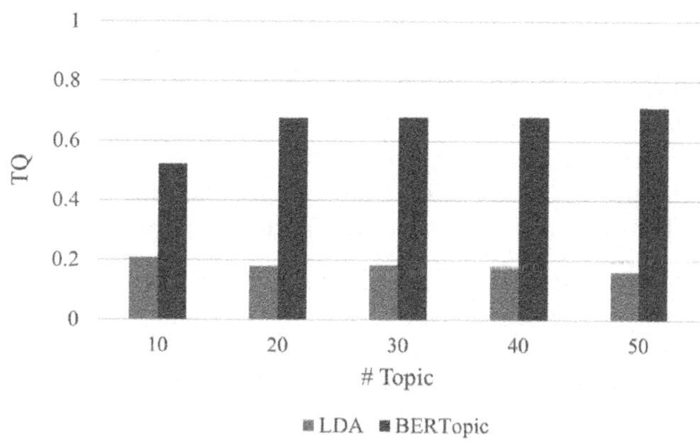

Fig. 10. Comparison of TQ.

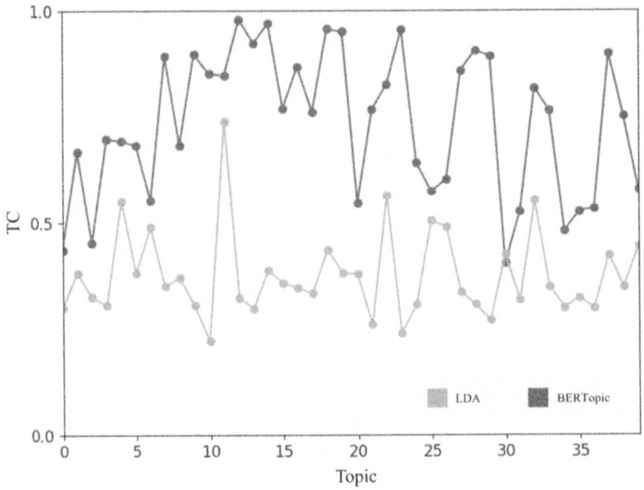

Fig. 11. TC scores for each of 40 topics.

in TQ across all topic quantities, indicating robustness in maintaining high-quality topics. This graph elucidates the responses of each algorithm to an array of topics, where BERTopic exhibits steadfast consistency, unlike the variability shown by LDA. These findings suggest a preference for BERTopic in applications of topic modeling, owing to its potential to enhance performance.

Figure 11 shows the TC score for 40 individual topics within the scope of LDA and BERTopic. Each line on the graph reflects the TC score changes corresponding to topic indices, with the vertical axis representing the TC values and the horizontal axis marking the topic numbers. LDA shows considerable fluctuation in TC scores, with some topics displaying notably lower consistency. Meanwhile, BERTopic consistently maintains higher TC values than those of LDA, signifying a superior level of topic consistency. Comparing the two models, BERTopic routinely achieves higher TC scores, implying the creation of topics with more robust and consistent semantic relations. The evidence suggests that BERTopic could outperform LDA in generating high-quality topics within the domain of topic modeling. The graph provides insights into the reaction of each topic modeling approach to the varied topics, underscoring the potential benefits of selecting BERTopic for enhanced topic modeling performance.

Qualitative Evaluation. We selected the top ten words for each of the forty topics derived through each methodology and visualized these words in word clouds, as shown in Figs. 12 and 13.

The results based on LDA uncover standard topic structures within the educational domain. In contrast, the results obtained through BERTopic reveal a greater diversity of topics, such as inclusive education, multimodal learning, and educational psychology. The LDA-based topic modeling prominently features

Fig. 12. Word clouds of LDA-based topic modeling.

terms such as 'eye' and 'gaze,' reflecting a focus on eye tracking within educational research. Results based on BERTopic display distinct boundaries between topics, delineating various sub-areas of the educational field.

Fig. 13. Word clouds of BERTopic-based topic modeling.

We also find that topics derived from BERTopic-based topic modeling show similarities with clustering outcomes from the scientometric analysis tool. Topic #1, comprising terms such as 'lecture' and 'instructor,' matches cluster ID 0 in CiteSpace, reflecting a concentration of research on teaching and instructors. Topic #0, featuring terms related to eye-tracking, aligns with CiteSpace cluster

ID 1. Topic #30, including terms like 'face' and 'video,' connects with cluster ID 2. Topic #3, concerning special education and attention, shows similarity to cluster ID 9, and Topic #17, encompassing mathematical and algorithmic modalities, corresponds with cluster ID 12.

When comparing with the institution-based CiteSpace analysis results, we observe that Topic #40, with terms such as 'facial' and 'expression,' could link to cluster ID 1, focusing on facial expression recognition research. Topic #39, containing terms like 'design' and 'vocational', shares similarities with cluster ID 9, which includes research in vocational education. The analysis confirms a meaningful correlation between the topics derived from the modeling and the clustering results from CiteSpace, suggesting that BERTopic effectively identifies and categorizes various topics in gaze-based educational research, thereby performing a complementary role to scientometric analysis.

BERTopic demonstrates its potential to contribute significantly to research analysis by providing meaningful topics, even in the absence of high semantical information. For example, topics generated from BERTopic show direct correspondence with CiteSpace clusters, affirming their effectiveness in detecting the interconnections among gaze-based educational topics and the evolving trends in academic networks. Comparative analyses like these aid in discovering principal topics and their impact on educational research, offering substantial insights into the educational dynamics and learning processes facilitated by human gaze data.

6 Discussion

By employing topic modeling methods based on LDA and BERTopic, alongside scientometric analysis, we identified topics and trends within gaze-based educational research published in the Web of Science from 2008 to 2024. Our analysis revealed a meaningful alignment between the topics uncovered through BERTopic-based topic modeling and the clusters obtained from scientometric analysis. Specifically, BERTopic effectively identified and categorized a diverse range of consistent topics in gaze-based educational research compared to LDA.

In the LDA, terms associated with 'eye' and 'gaze' prominently emerged. In contrast, BERTopic displayed clearly defined boundaries between topics, effectively revealing various sub-areas within the educational field. Each topic identified through BERTopic aligned with the clustering outcomes obtained through scientometric analysis. Significant topics such as inclusive education, multimodal learning, and educational psychology surfaced in both methods. These findings demonstrated the capability of BERTopic to effectively distinguish key topics, even without the high semantic information typical of scientometric analysis, thereby validating its crucial role in literature analysis.

Our findings highlighted the interconnectedness between gaze-based educational research and computer vision and underscored the potential for further collaboration and development. This study inspired prominent interdisciplinary approaches to more culturally inclusive and interactive visual learning interfaces across diverse educational settings and contexts.

Acknowledgements. This research was partly supported by Culture Technology R&D Program through the Korea Creative Content Agency grant funded by Ministry of Culture, Sports and Tourism in 2024 (Project Name: Development of Intelligent Heritage Platform for Leading of Standardization on Digital Cultural Heritage, Project Number: RS-2023-00219579), Institute of Information & communications Technology Planning & Evaluation (IITP) grant funded by the Korea government (MSIT) (2021-0-01341, Artificial Intelligence Graduate School Program (Chung-Ang University)), a grant (22193MFDS471) from the Ministry of Food and Drug Safety in 2024, and Social Sciences and Humanities Research Council (Insight Grant 435-2017-0179 & New Frontiers in Research Fund 2021-00302) & Internal Grants from Western University, Canada.

References

1. Blei, D.M., Ng, A.Y., Jordan, M.I.: Latent dirichlet allocation. J. Mach. Learn. Res. **3**, 993–1022 (2003)
2. Brown-Schmidt, S., Campana, E., Tanenhaus, M.K.: Real-time reference resolution by naïve participants during a task-based unscripted conversation. In: Approaches to Studying World-Situated Language Use: Bridging the Language-as-Product and Language-as-Action Traditions, pp. 153–171 (2005)
3. Casella, G., George, E.I.: Explaining the Gibbs sampler. Am. Stat. **46**(3), 167–174 (1992)
4. Chen, C.: Citespace (version 6.3.r1) (2024). http://cluster.cis.drexel.edu/cchen/citespace/
5. Chen, C.: CiteSpace II: detecting and visualizing emerging trends and transient patterns in scientific literature. J. Am. Soc. Inform. Sci. Technol. **57**(3), 359–377 (2006)
6. Dieng, A.B., Ruiz, F.J., Blei, D.M.: Topic modeling in embedding spaces. Trans. Assoc. Comput. Linguistics **8**, 439–453 (2020)
7. Grootendorst, M.: BERTopic: neural topic modeling with a class-based TF-IDF procedure. arXiv preprint arXiv:2203.05794 (2022)
8. Kim, M.S.: Developing a competency taxonomy for teacher design knowledge in technology-enhanced learning environments: a literature review. Res. Pract. Technol. Enhanced Learn. (2019)
9. Kim, M.S.: Deliberative collaboration in learning-by-designing multimodal modeling activities. Interact. Learn. Environ. **29**(8), 1319–1338 (2021)
10. Kingma, D.P., Welling, M.: Auto-encoding variational Bayes. arXiv preprint arXiv:1312.6114 (2013)
11. Kleinberg, J.: Bursty and hierarchical structure in streams. In: Proceedings of the Eighth ACM SIGKDD International Conference on Knowledge Discovery and Data Mining, pp. 91–101 (2002)
12. Liberati, A., et al.: The Prisma statement for reporting systematic reviews and meta-analyses of studies that evaluate health care interventions: explanation and elaboration. Ann. Internal Med. **151**(4), W–65 (2009)
13. Meng, Y., Zhang, Y., Huang, J., Zhang, Y., Han, J.: Topic discovery via latent space clustering of pretrained language model representations. In: Proceedings of the ACM Web Conference 2022, pp. 3143–3152 (2022)
14. Park, H., Kim, M.S., Ifewulu, H.A.: Reviewing design thinking in and out of education: scientometrics and visualization. Res. Integr. STEM Educ. **1**(2), 341–371 (2023)

15. Sia, S., Dalmia, A., Mielke, S.J.: Tired of topic models? Clusters of pretrained word embeddings make for fast and good topics too! arXiv preprint arXiv:2004.14914 (2020)
16. Srivastava, A., Sutton, C.: Autoencoding variational inference for topic models. arXiv preprint arXiv:1703.01488 (2017)
17. Wainwright, M.J., Jordan, M.I., et al.: Graphical models, exponential families, and variational inference. Found. Trends® Mach. Learn. **1**(1–2), 1–305 (2008)

Scientific Opinion Summarization: Paper Meta-review Generation Dataset, Methods, and Evaluation

Qi Zeng[1], Mankeerat Sidhu[1](✉), Ansel Blume[1], Hou Pong Chan[2], Lu Wang[3], and Heng Ji[1]

[1] University of Illinois Urbana-Champaign, Champaign, USA
{qizeng2,mssidhu2,blume5,hengji}@illinois.edu
[2] DAMO Academy, Alibaba Group, Hangzhou, China
houpong.chan@alibaba-inc.com
[3] University of Michigan, Ann Arbor, USA
wangluxy@umich.edu

Abstract. Opinions in scientific research papers can be divergent, leading to controversies among reviewers. However, most existing datasets for opinion summarization are centered around product reviews and assume that the analyzed opinions are non-controversial, failing to account for the variability seen in other contexts such as academic papers, political debates, or social media discussions. To address this gap, we propose the task of scientific opinion summarization, where research paper reviews are synthesized into meta-reviews. To facilitate this task, we introduce the ORSUM dataset covering 15,062 paper meta-reviews and 57,536 paper reviews from 47 conferences. Furthermore, we propose the Checklist-guided Iterative Introspection (CGI^2) approach, which breaks down scientific opinion summarization into several stages, iteratively refining the summary under the guidance of questions from a checklist. Our experiments show that (1) human-written summaries do not always satisfy all necessary criteria such as depth of discussion, and identifying consensus and controversy for the specific domain, and (2) the combination of task decomposition and iterative self-refinement shows strong potential for enhancing the opinions and can be applied to other complex text generation using black-box LLMs.

Keywords: Scientific Opinion Summarization · Meta-reviews · ORSUM dataset · Checklist-guided Iterative Introspection

1 Introduction

Opinion Summarization traditionally targets product reviews, aiming to distill representative opinions on key product aspects such as product quality and price.

Q. Zeng and M. Sidhu—Equal contribution.

W. Yin et al. (Eds.): IJCAI 2024, LNAI 14917, pp. 20–38, 2025.
https://doi.org/10.1007/978-981-97-9536-9_2

Domain	Reviews	Meta-reviews
Product	I love these protein bars in the vanilla flavor. They taste like Rice Krispies treats with vanilla frosting ... || Nugo bars are great for breakfast, lunch or a snack ... Eat them with a tall glass of water and they will keep you satisfied for hours. || ...	These bars are fantastic and taste great like a Rice Krispy treat. Good for morning, lunch or afternoon snack and a good way to get your protein in-take. They keep you full for a long time especially if you are out and about ...
Paper	It is unclear why this work is needed. Why not use ... || The paper is well written and the math seems to be sound ... The empirical evaluation of the method is not overwhelming ... || The work appears to be sound ...	Two of the reviews suggest that the technical aspects of the paper are sound, while one reviewer questions the need for the proposed approach ... While some reviewers raised concerns about ... the majority of reviewers acknowledge the ... In light of these findings, I recommend rejection ...

Fig. 1. Product meta-reviews and paper meta-reviews have different compositions: A product meta-review presents the most prominent opinion instead of summarizing opinions, while a paper meta-review summarizes different opinions and makes recommendations.

This assumes a dominant, singular opinion within the texts being summarized [2, 7, 29, 43]. However, this approach often overlooks the nuanced and multi-faceted nature of discussions in scientific documents, where multiple viewpoints may coexist and no single opinion dominates (Fig. 1).

Furthermore, most opinion summarization datasets in the product domain for abstractive summarization are synthetic, containing redundant cut-and-paste extracts built by combining extracted snippets, or by sampling a review from the collection and pretending that it is a gold-standard meta-review [2].

To address this gap, we introduce the new task of **Scientific Opinion Summarization**, where a set of opinions must be synthesized into a meta-opinion that justifies a decision. Scientific Opinion Summarization aims to provide a succinct synopsis for scientific documents, helping readers to recap salient information and understand the professional discussion. Scientific meta-reviews, in particular, summarize the *controversies* and *consensuses* in the reviews, guiding decision making such as the acceptance or rejection of a paper. Taking research paper meta-review generation as a typical scenario, we build the **ORSUM** dataset by collecting open-sourced paper and meta-reviews from OpenReview[1], covering 15,062 meta-reviews and 57,536 reviews from 47 conference venues. Compared to synthetic datasets from product review domains, ORSUM is built upon large-scale real-world data, enabling applications of supervised abstractive summarization methods and more fine-grained textual analysis. In addition to meta-review generation, ORSUM's structured content, including ratings

[1] https://openreview.net/.

on different aspects such as if agreements/disagreements are present alongside strengths/weaknesses and multi-turn discussions, will benefit a wide range of related tasks, such as review generation [45], recommendation prediction [20,24], review rating prediction [15,36], argument pair extraction [17], and argument generation [30].

The task of Scientific Opinion Summarization presents a distinct set of challenges, including (1) *Decision Consistency*: Whether the Meta-review aligns with the decision, which guides opinion selection and discussion in the meta-review. Generated scientific meta-reviews should reflect these decisions. (2) *Discussion involvement*: Unlike product meta-reviews that rely on majority voting, scientific meta-reviews assess both the pros and cons, as well as opinion agreement and disagreement, to evaluate the paper from the perspective of a more senior reviewer.

To tackle these challenges, we propose Checklist-guided Iterative Introspection (CGI^2). CGI^2 first breaks the task of scientific opinion summarization into multiple steps, constantly requesting evidence to mitigate both LLMs' inability to follow complicated instructions and their tendency to produce hallucinations. To enhance discussion involvement, CGI^2 iteratively revises the generated meta-review based on a predefined checklist. Finally, we identify key aspects a meta review should satisfy to be of high quality, and propose ways to evaluate these aspects using reference-free LLM-based metrics.

Our contributions include the following:

- We introduce the task of scientific opinion summarization and construct the ORSUM dataset, which contains 15,062 meta-reviews and 57,536 reviews from 47 conferences on OpenReview. It is currently the largest paper meta-review dataset.
- We propose Checklist-guided Iterative Introspection (CGI^2), which breaks down the task of scientific opinion summarization into several stages and iteratively refines the summary under the guidance of questions from a checklist.
- We construct a comprehensive evaluation framework for meta-review generation and assess the different summarization paradigms on ORSUM.

2 Related Work

2.1 Opinion Summarization

The task of opinion summarization is typically decomposed into three stages: aspect extraction, which identifies the specific features discussed in reviews; polarity identification, which assesses whether the sentiment towards each aspect is positive, negative, or neutral; and summary generation, which compiles these aspects and sentiments into a cohesive summary of the opinions [29]. The lack of parallel data in review summaries limits most methodologies into the few-shot abstractive setting [11,13], or unsupervised extractive setting [5,7,18] where the aspects and sentiments from the input reviews are collected, selected, and rearranged into the output meta-reviews.

Only a few previous opinion summarization datasets [44] contain gold-standard summaries and support supervised training of abstractive models [3]. Pretrained aspect-based sentiment analysis [43], variational autoencoders [12,19,31,32] and large language models [9] enable unsupervised abstractive approaches, where the generated summaries are validated to be more fluent, informative, coherent, and concise compared to traditional extractive summaries.

To support the training and evaluation of supervised methods, recent work constructs synthetic datasets by random sampling [42], adding noise to the sampled summary to generate documents [4], searching for relevant reviews to act as the input document set [22], or sampling with trained models [1,2]. However, synthetic pseudo-summaries in the product review domain are known to be detached from real-world distributions, be possibly irrelevant or inconsistent with input documents, and are known to ignore important underlying details.

2.2 Meta-review Generation

The first attempt to generate paper meta-reviews is MetaGen [10], which generates an extractive summary draft then uses a fine-tuned model for decision prediction and abstractive review generation. [34] emphasizes decision awareness, proposing a model for decision prediction and subsequent meta-review generation. The most similar work to ours is MReD [41], where 7,089 paper meta-reviews from ICLR 2018–2021 are manually annotated with sentence-level structure labels. These structure labels categorize sentences based on their function in the document, such as summary, evaluation, or recommendation. The difference between their work and ours is that they focus on structure-controlled text generation, while our work 1) enables scientific opinion summarization with a larger corpus, 2) provides a prompting-based solution, and 3) performs broader evaluations. Note that while there are other concurrent efforts to collect paper meta-reviews or reviews [21], we are the first to model meta-review generation as scientific opinion summarization and to offer a unified dataset covering a broad range of conference venues.

3 Task Formulation

Given a research paper's title, abstract, and set of reviews, the goal of **Scientific Opinion Summarization** is to generate a meta-review summarizing the reviews' opinions in order to make a decision recommendation for acceptance or rejection.

As noted by ACL's area chair guidance[2], meta-reviews summarize reviews by aggregating opinions to support the decision. The task entails summarizing the paper's key strengths and weaknesses and explicitly evaluating whether those strengths surpass the weaknesses.

[2] https://aclrollingreview.org/aetutorial.

Table 1. Comparison of ORSUM with existing opinion summarization datasets that contain gold-standard summaries. SRC refers to the source or input reviews. TRG refers to the target or output meta-reviews. A higher Novel 4-gram score suggests better abstractiveness, while a lower NID score implies less redundancy.

Dataset	Collection	Count(SRC)	Count(TRG)	Len(SRC)	Len(TRG)	Novel 4-gram	NID
RT	Human	246,164	3,731	20.57	21.4	97.10	0.1615
Copycat	AMT	480	180	42.63	54.33	89.62	0.2506
OPOSUM	AMT	600	60	43.51	67.77	85.92	0.1260
Yelp	AMT	3,200	200	65.25	61.15	93.26	0.1661
DENOISESUM	Synthetic	73,282	837	24.32	26.45	94.12	0.2270
PLANSUM	Synthetic	249,844	869	42.81	97.2	91.40	0.2395
SPACE	Human	5,000	1,050	34.27	54.38	90.38	0.1671
ORSUM	Human	57,536	15,062	376.36	141.76	99.89	0.1572

4 ORSUM Dataset

4.1 Dataset Collection and Preprocessing

To facilitate the task of scientific opinion summarization, we collect the **ORSUM** dataset which consists of human-written meta-reviews from OpenReview. The dataset contains each paper's URL, title, abstract, decision, meta-review from the area chair, and reviews from individual reviewers. We crawl 15,062 paper meta-reviews and 57,536 individual reviews from 47 conference venues. Papers with meta-reviews shorter than 20 tokens and comments made by non-official reviewers are excluded. The data format is unified across venues, and we provide train/validation/test splits with 9,890/549/550 samples for convenient usage by future works.

4.2 Dataset Comparison

We compare ORSUM with existing opinion summarization datasets (or their subsets) with gold-standard summaries, including The Rotten Tomatoes (RT) [44], Copycat [12], OPOSUM [7], Yelp [19], DENOISESUM [4], PLANSUM [2], and SPACE [6] datasets. To perform a quantitative comparison, we utilize two key metrics:

Abstractiveness. The percentage of novel n-grams in a meta-review is defined by the ratio of n-grams which do not appear in the source reviews, to the total number of n-grams in the meta review. This metric intuitively measures the abstractiveness of the summaries [16]. Table 1 indicates a greater degree of abstractiveness in ORSUM.

Redundancy. To examine the presence of insightful information in the input reviews, we assess redundancy using the Normalized Inverse of Diversity (NID) score [46] This score is calculated as the inverse of the diversity metric, which measures the variability of information in the reviews with length normalization: $NID = 1 - \frac{(entropy(D)}{log(|D|)}$. A higher NID signifies greater redundancy. Table 1 shows lower redundancy in ORSUM, which can be attributed to the fact that many reviews address distinct aspects of their papers.

4.3 Composition Analysis

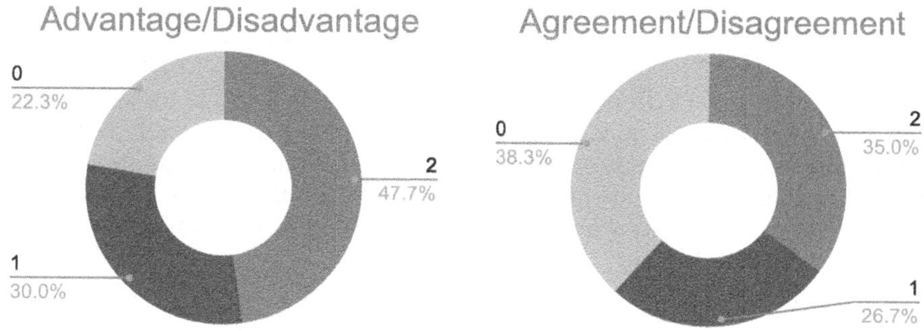

Fig. 2. Meta-review composition. The scores range from 0 to 2: 0 indicates that the meta-review does not address the discussion at all. 1 signifies that the meta-review incorporates the discussion but lacks concrete evidence. 2 denotes that the meta-review involves a detailed discussion. Only 47.7% and 35.0% of meta-reviews meet the fundamental criteria for discussions of advantages and disadvantages, and consensus and controversy, respectively.

To investigate whether ORSUM's human-authored meta-reviews discuss both a paper's pros/cons and the reviews' level of agreement/disagreement, we conduct a human evaluation focused on meta-review composition. Three annotators are asked to assess the meta-reviews in terms of **discussion involvement**: how effectively a summary engages with the content by discussing the paper's advantages/disadvantages, and by discussing the agreements/disagreements of the reviews. Annotation scores range from 0 (no involvement) to 2 (detailed involvement).

Our evaluation results depicted in Fig. 2 reveal that only 20.7% of meta-reviews include an assessment of both advantages/disadvantages and review agreements/disagreements, regardless of their length. For each category, 47.7%, and 35.0% of meta-reviews meet the criteria of containing discussions of advantages and disadvantages and discussions of agreements/disagreements, respectively. Based on these results, we conclude that *human-written meta-reviews do not always meet the necessary criteria for an effective meta review, and they may be unsuitable for developing summarization models as supervised training signals. The low percentage of comprehensive reviews highlights a gap in coverage and thoroughness that can affect the performance and reliability of models trained on these summaries.*

5 Checklist-Guided Iterative Introspection Method for Meta-review Generation

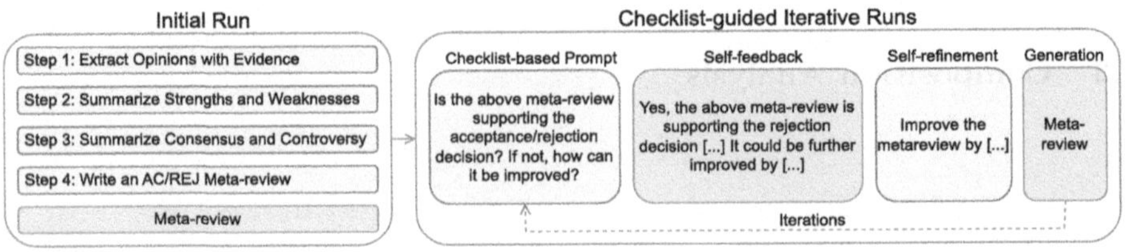

Fig. 3. Our proposed CGI^2 framework operates through multiple iterations. In the initial iteration, the task is divided into four steps: (1) Review Opinion Extraction, (2) Strength and Weakness Synthesis, (3) Consensus and Controversy Analysis, and (4) Meta-review Drafting. For subsequent iterations, we present the black-box LLM with a query from a predefined list, acquire self-feedback, and request additional refinements.

Table 2. The extensible and easily adaptable checklist for Meta-review Generation accesses the essential aspects of self-consistency, faithfulness, and active engagement in discussions.

1. Are the most important advantages and disadvantages discussed in the above meta-review? If not, how can it be improved?
2. Are the most important consensus and controversy discussed in the above meta-review? If not, how can it be improved?
3. Is the above meta-review contradicting reviewers' comments? If so, how can it be improved?
4. Is the above meta-review supporting the acceptance/rejection decision? If not, how can it be improved?

Motivated by the unreliability of human-written meta-reviews, we turn to Large Language Models (LLMs) like ChatGPT [40] for meta-review generation. We choose LLMs for their world knowledge, and their potential to generate reviews efficiently and scalably. However, LLMs struggle to follow complicated instructions, and have a tendency to produce hallucinations. To mitigate these deficiencies, we propose to break the task of scientific review generation into multiple steps, consistently requesting evidence for each step. To enhance discussion involvement and evidence-based coherence in the generation process, we further introduce a checklist-guided self-feedback mechanism. Our method is similar to the process of self-refinement [39], which involves the LLM iteratively revising the generated meta-review based on its own feedback. Unlike prior work, however, our checklist-guided self-feedback uses self-feedback derived from questions in a predefined checklist, ensuring that the revision process progresses towards our desired criteria. Figure 3 illustrates our proposed Checklist-guided Iterative Introspection (CGI^2) method.

Initial Run. Given a paper's title, abstract, and set of reviews, CGI^2 generates a draft of the meta-review in four steps: (1) For each review, we prompt the LLM to extract and rank opinions, while including sentiment, aspect, and evidence. Due to the input length constraint, each review is truncated to 300 tokens. (2) Based on the extracted opinions, we prompt the LLM to list the paper's most important advantages and disadvantages, the evidence for those statements, and those statements' corresponding reviewers. (3) We prompt the LLM to list the consensuses and controversies in the reviews, the evidence for those statements, and their corresponding reviewers. (4) Given the paper's acceptance or rejection decision, we prompt the LLM to write a meta-review based on the information extracted in steps (1)–(3).

Iterative Runs. With the meta-review draft from the initial four-step run, CGI^2 iteratively poses questions, obtains self-feedback, and requests further refinement. In each run, we first select an assessment question from a pre-constructed list of questions, as shown in Table 2. This checklist, customized for meta-review generation, covers the four most crucial aspects of meta-reviews. The checklist can also easily be expanded and adapted to other complex text generation tasks. After prompting the LLM with the assessment questions, we collect the refinement suggestions from the LLM's. These refinement suggestions are used as prompts to generate a revised version of the meta-review. The checklist questions are posed sequentially in one iterative run, with the number of iterations set as a hyper-parameter in CGI^2.

Our proposed approach offers two key benefits. First, it eliminates the need for external scoring functions that demand training data or human annotations. Second, it provides a general solution for employing LLMs as black boxes in complex text generation tasks.

6 Evaluation

Meta-review generation requires a system to accurately summarize opinions, highlight reviewer consensuses and controversies, offer judgments, and make recommendations. The task's complexity thus requires an evaluation that is multi-faceted and goes beyond n-gram similarity. However, current evaluation metrics for long text generation are inadequate to measure the particular requirements of meta-review generation. To address this gap, we propose a comprehensive evaluation framework that combines standard evaluation metrics with LLM-based evaluation metrics.

6.1 Standard Metrics

We apply standard metrics in natural language generation to assess *relevance*, *factual consistency*, and *semantic coherence*. For relevance, ROUGE-L [37] quantifies the similarity between the generated and reference texts by calculating the longest common subsequence, while BERTScore [47] offers a more nuanced relevance evaluation by leveraging contextualized embeddings without relying on n-gram overlaps. For factual consistency, FACTCC [33] checks whether a given claim in the generated text is consistent with the facts presented in the source

G-EVAL

You will be given one metareview written for reviews by the committee on a paper. Your task is to rate the metareview on one metric. Please make sure you read and understand these instructions carefully. Please keep this document open while reviewing, and refer to it as needed.
Evaluation Criteria: Quality of Metareview (1-5) - the collective quality of all sentences. We align this dimension with the DUC quality question of structure and coherence whereby the metareview should be well-structured and well-organized. The metareview should always discuss the disadvantages and advantages of a paper and have a clear scope of the accept/reject decision. The metareview should have concrete evidence from the papers reviews and concrete comments as well.
Evaluation Steps:
1. Read the reviews carefully and identify the main topic and key points.
2. Read the metareview and compare it to the reviews. Check if the metareview covers the main topic, discusses advantages and disadvantages, if the most important advantages and disadvantages discussed in the above meta-review, if the most important advantages and disadvantages discussed in the above meta-review, if the most important consensus and controversy discussed in the above meta-review, if the above meta-review contradicting reviewers' comments, if the above meta-review supporting the acceptance/rejection decision, and if it presents them in a clear and logical order.
3. Assign a score for the quality of the meta-review on a scale of 1 to 5, where 1 is the lowest and 5 is the highest based on the Evaluation Criteria.
Source Text: {Reviews} Metareview: {Meta-review} Evaluation Form (scores ONLY): - Quality of metareview :

Likert scale scoring with ChatGPT

Imagine you are a human annotator now. You will evaluate the quality of metareviews written for a conference by giving a mean value from 1 to 5 and no other explanation. Please follow these steps:
1. Carefully read the reviews, and be aware of the information it contains.
2. Read the proposed metareview.
3. Rate the summary on three dimensions: 'Discussion Involvement', 'Opinion Faithfulness' and 'Decision Consistency'. You should rate on a scale from 1 (worst) to 5 (best) and give me an average of these scores over all aspects from 1 to 5 calculated by the mean of all aspects.
Definitions are as follows:
(1) Discussion Involvement: Whether the meta-review discusses the paper's strengths and weaknesses, as well as agreements and disagreements among reviewers,
(2) Opinion Faithfulness: Whether the meta-review contradicts reviewers' comments,
(3) Decision Consistency: Whether the meta-review accurately reflects the final decisions.
Only generate the mean rating as a number on the likert scale, nothing else.

Fig. 4. We customize the prompts in G-EVAL and GPTLikert for evaluating meta-review generation to assess discussion involvement, opinion faithfulness, and decision consistency.

document, while SummaC [35] utilizes sentence-level natural language inference models for inconsistency detection. For semantic coherence, DiscoScore [48] presents six BERT-based model variants to measure discourse coherence. We average the scores from these six models as the coherence indicator. The references used in our reference-free evaluation metrics are sourced from a test subset of our dataset, where the instances are chosen for their relevance and quality. These references provide a practical benchmark that mirrors current standards in meta-review generation at top conferences.

6.2 LLM-Based Metrics

The aforementioned methods do not evaluate discussion involvement or evidence-decision consistency. Some reference summaries may not include discussions or utilize evidence to substantiate decisions. To address this, we propose supplementary measures for this task that can be assessed and quantified using reference-free LLM-based metrics. We aim to assess the following key aspects:

- Discussion involvement: whether the meta-review discusses the paper's strengths and weaknesses, and the paper's agreements and disagreements amongst reviewers.
- Opinion Faithfulness: whether the meta-review contradicts reviewers' opinions.
- Decision Consistency: whether the meta-review accurately reflects the final decision.

Despite its prevalence, the GPTScore [25] metric requires its criteria to be described as a single word, a requirement incompatible with our detailed criteria. On the other hand, G-EVAL [38] assesses the quality of NLG outputs by utilizing chain-of-thought (CoT) and a form-filling paradigm. It has been shown to have a very high correlation with human-based judgments. G-EVAL uses carefully constructed instructions for GPT models to follow, yielding a rating on the Likert scale ranging from 1 to 5. Likert scoring with ChatGPT (GPTLikert), a human-like evaluation method introduced by [26], follows a similar evaluation protocol, outperforming many standard metrics on text summarization as measured by human correlation. We are the first to adapt these methods to meta-review generation by modifying the prompts as shown in Fig. 4. The combination of standard metrics like ROUGE-L and BERTScore with LLM-based metrics such as G-EVAL and GPTLikert ensures a comprehensive evaluation, capturing nuances that traditional metrics may overlook. This multifaceted approach not only adheres to current evaluation methodologies, but also enhances them by introducing metrics that demonstrate a high correlation with human annotations.

7 Experiments

Table 3. ROUGE-L and BERTScore assess semantic similarity with reference text. FactCC and SummaC detect factual consistency. DiscoScore measures coherence. G-EVAL and GPTLikert are GPT-based comprehensive evaluation measures for discussion involvement, opinion faithfulness, and decision consistency.

Models	ROUGE-L	BERTScore	FactCC	SummaC	DiscoScore	G-EVAL	GPTLikert
Human	-	-	0.538	0.368	0.740	0.731	0.607
Abstractive Methods							
PlanSum	**0.465**	0.785	0.608	0.533	0.911	0.731	0.608
OpinionDigest	0.124	0.838	0.612	0.575	0.862	0.762	0.618
MeanSum	0.132	0.827	0.559	0.464	0.900	0.767	0.622
LED	0.161	0.846	0.618	0.785	0.958	0.731	0.624
LED-finetuned	0.221	0.853	0.634	0.795	0.961	0.751	0.649
Extractive Methods							
LexRank	0.433	**0.881**	**0.729**	**0.937**	**1.256**	0.726	0.656
MemSum	0.337	0.827	0.683	0.825	0.989	0.711	0.628
Prompting Methods							
Vanilla	0.174	0.817	0.498	0.423	0.808	0.752	0.626
3Sent	0.109	0.783	0.562	0.503	0.667	0.758	0.661
InstructPrompt	0.208	0.823	0.543	0.449	0.862	0.751	0.646
TCG	0.189	0.847	0.544	0.466	0.895	0.761	0.632
ICL	0.192	0.847	0.578	0.470	0.871	0.756	0.612
CGI^2 (ours)	0.199	0.836	0.559	0.320	0.906	**0.770**	**0.687**
CGI^2 w/o Iterative Runs	0.118	0.830	0.536	0.332	0.849	0.732	0.629

Human

The paper unanimously receives positive rates thanks to strong motivations and interesting results. As the reviews show satisfaction on the authors' feedback, the final draft needs to respect it accordingly, for example, about the limitations of this research.

Vanilla

This paper could have benefited from a clearer and more concise presentation of the main findings. It is sometimes difficult to follow the paper's chain of thought, and the authors could have presented their results in a more accessible way. The experiments are limited to a small set of environments, and it would be interesting to see how the results generalize to other tasks. Additionally, it would be useful to have a deeper analysis of why iGPT does not perform well, as this could help inform future research on how to improve image-based pretraining.

CGI^2

After carefully considering the reviews provided, there is consensus that the paper presents an important and thought-provoking analysis of representation dynamics between pretraining and finetuning in the context of reinforcement learning. Both reviewers agree that the paper addresses an important question and presents insightful experiments. One reviewer highlights the experiments as a strong point in the paper, while the other reviewer raises a concern about the paper's tendency to present hypotheses without exploring them further.

Overall, the strengths of the paper outweigh its weaknesses, and it has the potential to make a significant contribution to the field of reinforcement learning. Therefore, I recommend accepting the paper with a minor revision to address the concern raised by the reviewer. Specifically, the paper should explore the hypotheses presented in more depth to provide a more comprehensive analysis. If the authors can address this concern, the paper can make a valuable contribution to the field of reinforcement learning.

In summary, I recommend accepting the paper with a minor revision.

Initial run

Based on the reviews, I recommend accepting the paper. The paper addresses an important and under-explored research question and presents a detailed and thought-provoking analysis of the pretraining-finetuning paradigm for Transformer models in the context of reinforcement learning. The paper also identifies relevant techniques to perform analysis of representation similarity and training dynamics. While there are some weaknesses pointed out, such as the need for further exploration of some hypotheses and occasional difficulty in following the writing and presentation, the strengths of the paper outweigh these concerns. Therefore, I recommend accepting the paper with minor revisions to address the weaknesses pointed out by the reviewers.

Fig. 5. We show the meta-reviews from human, vanilla, CGI^2, and CGI^2 without iterative runs for the same paper. The yellow background indicates hallucinated content. The green background indicates redundant content. (Color figure online)

Table 4. Human annotation results on meta-reviews for 50 challenging papers from the test set.

Model	Informativeness	Soundness	Self-consistency	Faithfulness
Human	0.71	0.68	0.67	-
LED-finetuned	0.56	0.46	0.21	0.73
LexRank	0.87	0.94	0.16	-
CGI^2 (ours)	**0.98**	**0.92**	**0.84**	**0.79**
CGI^2 w/o Iterative Runs	0.97	0.76	0.48	0.74

7.1 Baselines

We compare our proposed CGI^2 method with methods of different paradigms. Results in Table 3 are averaged across three random runs.

Abstractive Methods. PlanSum [2] uses a Condense-Abstract Framework, where reviews are condensed and used as input to an abstractive summarization model. OpinionDigest [43] extracts opinions from input reviews and trains a seq2seq model that generates a summary from this set of opinions. MeanSum [19] is an unsupervised multi-document abstractive summarizer that minimizes a combination of reconstruction and vector similarity losses. LED [8] is a Longformer [8] variant supporting long document generative sequence-to-sequence tasks.

Extractive Methods. LexRank [23] is an unsupervised extractive summarization method that selects sentences based on centrality scores calculated with graph-based sentence similarity. MemSum [28] models extractive summarization as a multi-step episodic Markov Decision Process of scoring and selecting sentences.

Prompting Methods. All prompting methods are initiated with the GPT-3.5-turbo model with a temperature of 0.7. 3Sent [27] applies a simple prompt "Summary of document in 3 sentences". TCG [9] explores a four-step generation pipeline involving topic classification, sentence grouping by topic, generating chunk-wise summary, and generating the final summary. We also explore In Context Learning (ICL) [14], where a highly rated meta-review alongside the reviews is given as part of the model's prompt. This meta-review is manually picked based on adherence to the previously defined checklist, and is chosen for its fulfillment of the criteria that define a high-quality meta-review. Vanilla uses "Generate a metareview" as the prompt. InstructPrompt provides more detailed step by step instructions and specifies the criteria for writing a metareview.

7.2 Automatic Evaluation

Higher standard metric scores indicate better summarization, but not necessarily better opinion summarization. ROUGE-L, BERTScore, SummaC, and DiscoScore do not consider the multifaceted nature of meta-review, which goes beyond summarization. Our method performs near average in BERTScore and SummaC, and the highest in ROUGE-L and DiscoScore amongst the prompting methods. Compared to extractive and abstractive methods, our method achieves lower scores as some metrics measure semantic similarity which a high-quality measure review with its variability may not score well in. Additionally due to the multifaceted nature of opinion summarization, reference-based metrics such as Rouge-L can be biased towards the reference, thus the elevated scores of the summarization methods.

Evaluators like G-Eval and GPTLikert favor specific dimensions given in their prompts. Our method shows promising results in both G-Eval and GPTLikert due to the carefully constructed and revised prompts. Most prompting methods also outperform extractive and abstractive methods.

Human meta-reviews in the dataset scored among the lowest in all categories, signifying the unreliability of some human-written meta-reviews and the need for an automatic, or auxiliary, writing process. When compared by semantic similarity, extractive methods outperform both abstractive and prompting methods with the exception of Plansum. This is due to the nature of content planning in Plansum which is central to the task of meta-review generation.

7.3 Human Evaluation

We conduct a human annotation on 50 challenging papers from the test set which have average review scores on the borderline of acceptance. Five anonymized outputs from Human, LED-finetuned, LexRank, CGI^2, and CGI^2 without iterative runs, are shown to three annotators. Annotators are asked to provide binary labels for informativeness, soundness, self-consistency, and faithfulness for each meta-review. Informativeness measures whether the meta-review involves a discussion of both strengths and weaknesses. Soundness examines whether the meta-review provides evidence to support the discussed strengths and weaknesses. Decision consistency indicates whether the recommendation decision is clearly written and consistent with the comments in the meta-review. Faithfulness evaluates whether the meta-review contains hallucinations. We assume Human and the extractive LexRank framework have perfectly faithful summaries.

Results shown in Table 4 validate the effectiveness of our proposed method. The extractive method (LexRank) is easily biased toward one reviewer and involves no discussion or decision, but generates no hallucinations by construction. The abstractive method (LED-finetuned) learns to copy the sentences in the input and form a short meta-review with little discussion, sometimes hallucinating or generating repetitive outputs. Our prompting-based method exhibits less hallucination due to the evidence requirements in our prompts. Compared to human-written meta-reviews, all automatic methods are less capable of generating in-depth analyses, a deficiency which calls for knowledge enhancement that happens a LLM enhanced with reviews.

We also observe that hallucinations in LLMs are more likely to happen when summarizing consensuses and controversies, which require information from the paper itself. By contrast, the abstractive methods' hallucinations were are more likely to be general comments, whereas extractive methods tend to misrepresent the context by selecting irrelevant or less important sections. Despite our method's improvements in this area, hallucination detection for scientific opinion summarization remains an open problem.

7.4 Case Study

Figure 5 presents the meta-reviews from human, vanilla, CGI^2, and CGI^2 without iterative runs for a random paper[3].

We make the following general observations: (1) The hallucination problem is alleviated in CGI^2 as the model is constantly asked for evidence. (2) CGI^2's summary sentences are redundant. (3) The vanilla prompting baseline does not make recommendations and involve discussion, as the model fails to fully understand the complex task requirement. (4) Iterative refinement sometimes improves the concreteness of opinion discussion. However, there are two problems with iterative refinements. First, suggestions provided by the large language model are usually generic and less useful for further refinement. Second, more self-refinement iterations cause the model to forget the initial instructions for opinion extraction and discussion.

8 Conclusions and Future Work

In this paper, we introduced the task of scientific opinion summarization, in which research paper reviews are synthesized into meta-reviews. To facilitate this task, we introduce the ORSUM dataset, an evaluation framework, and an approach that we call Checklist-Guided Iterative Introspection. We conduct an empirical analysis of methods from different paradigms, concluding that human-written summaries do not always satisfy the criteria of an ideal meta-review, and that the combination of task decomposition and iterative self-refinement shows promise in on this task.

Direct extensions of this work include the incorporation of author rebuttals into the input data to enhance the model's ability to generate more balanced meta-reviews, and introducing an effective and efficient hallucination detection tool for scientific opinion summarization.

Limitations

This work on scientific opinion summarization has limitations in terms of data scope and task configuration. As the dataset is collected from OpenReview, the majority of meta-reviews are in Machine Learning, and many papers have been accepted. Conclusions drawn from this data distribution might not be applicable to datasets in other domains. Furthermore, to simplify the task setting, author rebuttals have not been included as input, which may also constrain the extent of discussion involvement in generating meta-reviews.

[3] https://openreview.net/forum?id=9GXoMs__ckJ.

Acknowledgements. This research is based upon work supported by U.S. DARPA AIDA Program No. FA8750-18-2-0014, DARPA INCAS Program No. HR001121C0165, NSF under award No. 2034562, the Molecule Maker Lab Institute: an AI research institute program supported by NSF under award No. 2019897 and No. 2034562, and the AI Research Institutes program by National Science Foundation and the Institute of Education Sciences, U.S. Department of Education through Award # 2229873 - AI Institute for Transforming Education for Children with Speech and Language Processing Challenges. The views and conclusions contained herein are those of the authors and should not be interpreted as necessarily representing the official policies, either expressed or implied, of the U.S. Government, the National Science Foundation, the Institute of Education Sciences, or the U.S. Department of Education. The U.S. Government is authorized to reproduce and distribute reprints for governmental purposes notwithstanding any copyright annotation therein.

Ethics Statement. We acknowledge the following potential ethical concerns that may arise. First, the meta-reviews generated by LLMs may contain hallucinations, which may lead to misunderstandings of the original research paper or reviewers' opinions. Therefore, users should be cautious when using system-generated meta-reviews for recommendation decisions. Second, the use of black-box LLMs for meta-review generation may raise concerns about the transparency of the decision process. Though our method improves explainability by prompting an LLM to provide supporting evidence for the recommendation decision, the evidence may not perfectly reflect the decision-making process. Third, the dataset used in this study mainly focuses on machine learning papers, which could introduce biases to the recommendation decisions. Hence, it is critical to consider these biases when applying our method to generate meta-reviews for research papers in other domains.

References

1. Amplayo, R.K., Angelidis, S., Lapata, M.: Aspect-controllable opinion summarization. In: Proceedings of the 2021 Conference on Empirical Methods in Natural Language Processing, pp. 6578–6593. Association for Computational Linguistics, Online and Punta Cana, Dominican Republic, November 2021. https://doi.org/10.18653/v1/2021.emnlp-main.528. https://aclanthology.org/2021.emnlp-main.528
2. Amplayo, R.K., Angelidis, S., Lapata, M.: Unsupervised opinion summarization with content planning. In: Thirty-Fifth AAAI Conference on Artificial Intelligence, AAAI 2021, Thirty-Third Conference on Innovative Applications of Artificial Intelligence, IAAI 2021, The Eleventh Symposium on Educational Advances in Artificial Intelligence, EAAI 2021, Virtual Event, 2–9 February 2021, pp. 12489–12497. AAAI Press (2021). https://doi.org/10.1609/AAAI.V35I14.17481
3. Amplayo, R.K., Lapata, M.: Informative and controllable opinion summarization. CoRR abs/1909.02322 (2019). http://arxiv.org/abs/1909.02322
4. Amplayo, R.K., Lapata, M.: Unsupervised opinion summarization with noising and denoising. In: Jurafsky, D., Chai, J., Schluter, N., Tetreault, J.R. (eds.) Proceedings of the 58th Annual Meeting of the Association for Computational Linguistics, ACL 2020, Online, 5–10 July 2020, pp. 1934–1945. Association for Computational Linguistics (2020). https://doi.org/10.18653/v1/2020.acl-main.175

5. Angelidis, S., Amplayo, R.K., Suhara, Y., Wang, X., Lapata, M.: Extractive opinion summarization in quantized transformer spaces. CoRR abs/2012.04443 (2020). https://arxiv.org/abs/2012.04443
6. Angelidis, S., Amplayo, R.K., Suhara, Y., Wang, X., Lapata, M.: Extractive opinion summarization in quantized transformer spaces. Trans. Assoc. Comput. Linguist. **9**, 277–293 (2021). https://doi.org/10.1162/tacl_a_00366. https://aclanthology.org/2021.tacl-1.17
7. Angelidis, S., Lapata, M.: Summarizing opinions: aspect extraction meets sentiment prediction and they are both weakly supervised. In: Riloff, E., Chiang, D., Hockenmaier, J., Tsujii, J. (eds.) Proceedings of the 2018 Conference on Empirical Methods in Natural Language Processing, Brussels, Belgium, 31 October–4 November 2018, pp. 3675–3686. Association for Computational Linguistics (2018). https://doi.org/10.18653/v1/d18-1403
8. Beltagy, I., Peters, M.E., Cohan, A.: Longformer: the long-document transformer. CoRR abs/2004.05150 (2020). https://arxiv.org/abs/2004.05150
9. Bhaskar, A., Fabbri, A.R., Durrett, G.: Zero-shot opinion summarization with GPT-3. CoRR abs/2211.15914 (2022). https://doi.org/10.48550/arXiv.2211.15914
10. Bhatia, C., Pradhan, T., Pal, S.: MetaGen: an academic meta-review generation system. In: Huang, J.X., et al. (eds.) Proceedings of the 43rd International ACM SIGIR Conference on Research and Development in Information Retrieval, SIGIR 2020, Virtual Event, China, 25–30 July 2020, pp. 1653–1656. ACM (2020). https://doi.org/10.1145/3397271.3401190
11. Brazinskas, A., Lapata, M., Titov, I.: Few-shot learning for opinion summarization. In: Webber, B., Cohn, T., He, Y., Liu, Y. (eds.) Proceedings of the 2020 Conference on Empirical Methods in Natural Language Processing, EMNLP 2020, Online, 16–20 November 2020, pp. 4119–4135. Association for Computational Linguistics (2020). https://doi.org/10.18653/v1/2020.emnlp-main.337
12. Brazinskas, A., Lapata, M., Titov, I.: Unsupervised opinion summarization as copycat-review generation. In: Jurafsky, D., Chai, J., Schluter, N., Tetreault, J.R. (eds.) Proceedings of the 58th Annual Meeting of the Association for Computational Linguistics, ACL 2020, Online, 5–10 July 2020, pp. 5151–5169. Association for Computational Linguistics (2020). https://doi.org/10.18653/v1/2020.acl-main.461
13. Brazinskas, A., Nallapati, R., Bansal, M., Dreyer, M.: Efficient few-shot fine-tuning for opinion summarization. In: Carpuat, M., de Marneffe, M., Ruíz, I.V.M. (eds.) Findings of the Association for Computational Linguistics: NAACL 2022, Seattle, WA, United States, 10–15 July 2022, pp. 1509–1523. Association for Computational Linguistics (2022). https://doi.org/10.18653/v1/2022.findings-naacl.113
14. Brown, T.B., et al.: Language models are few-shot learners. In: Larochelle, H., Ranzato, M., Hadsell, R., Balcan, M., Lin, H. (eds.) Advances in Neural Information Processing Systems 33: Annual Conference on Neural Information Processing Systems 2020, NeurIPS 2020, 6–12 December 2020, Virtual (2020). https://proceedings.neurips.cc/paper/2020/hash/1457c0d6bfcb4967418bfb8ac142f64a-Abstract.html
15. Chan, H.P., Chen, W., King, I.: A unified dual-view model for review summarization and sentiment classification with inconsistency loss. In: Huang, J.X., et al. (eds.) Proceedings of the 43rd International ACM SIGIR Conference on Research and Development in Information Retrieval, SIGIR 2020, Virtual Event, China, 25–30 July 2020, pp. 1191–1200. ACM (2020). https://doi.org/10.1145/3397271.3401039

16. Chen, Y., Liu, Y., Chen, L., Zhang, Y.: DialogSum: a real-life scenario dialogue summarization dataset. In: Zong, C., Xia, F., Li, W., Navigli, R. (eds.) Findings of the Association for Computational Linguistics: ACL/IJCNLP 2021, Online Event, 1–6 August 2021. Findings of ACL, ACL/IJCNLP 2021, pp. 5062–5074. Association for Computational Linguistics (2021). https://doi.org/10.18653/v1/2021.findings-acl.449
17. Cheng, L., Bing, L., Yu, Q., Lu, W., Si, L.: APE: argument pair extraction from peer review and rebuttal via multi-task learning. In: Webber, B., Cohn, T., He, Y., Liu, Y. (eds.) Proceedings of the 2020 Conference on Empirical Methods in Natural Language Processing, EMNLP 2020, Online, 16–20 November 2020, pp. 7000–7011. Association for Computational Linguistics (2020). https://doi.org/10.18653/v1/2020.emnlp-main.569
18. Chowdhury, S.B.R., Zhao, C., Chaturvedi, S.: Unsupervised extractive opinion summarization using sparse coding. In: Muresan, S., Nakov, P., Villavicencio, A. (eds.) Proceedings of the 60th Annual Meeting of the Association for Computational Linguistics (Volume 1: Long Papers), ACL 2022, Dublin, Ireland, 22–27 May 2022, pp. 1209–1225. Association for Computational Linguistics (2022). https://doi.org/10.18653/v1/2022.acl-long.86
19. Chu, E., Liu, P.J.: MeanSum: a neural model for unsupervised multi-document abstractive summarization. In: Chaudhuri, K., Salakhutdinov, R. (eds.) Proceedings of the 36th International Conference on Machine Learning, ICML 2019, 9–15 June 2019, Long Beach, California, USA. Proceedings of Machine Learning Research, vol. 97, pp. 1223–1232. PMLR (2019). http://proceedings.mlr.press/v97/chu19b.html
20. Deng, Z., Peng, H., Xia, C., Li, J., He, L., Yu, P.S.: Hierarchical bi-directional self-attention networks for paper review rating recommendation. In: Scott, D., Bel, N., Zong, C. (eds.) Proceedings of the 28th International Conference on Computational Linguistics, COLING 2020, Barcelona, Spain (Online), 8–13 December 2020, pp. 6302–6314. International Committee on Computational Linguistics (2020).https://doi.org/10.18653/v1/2020.coling-main.555
21. Dycke, N., Kuznetsov, I., Gurevych, I.: NLPeer: a unified resource for the computational study of peer review. In: Rogers, A., Boyd-Graber, J., Okazaki, N. (eds.) Proceedings of the 61st Annual Meeting of the Association for Computational Linguistics (Volume 1: Long Papers), pp. 5049–5073. Association for Computational Linguistics, Toronto, Canada, July 2023. https://doi.org/10.18653/v1/2023.acl-long.277
22. Elsahar, H., Coavoux, M., Rozen, J., Gallé, M.: Self-supervised and controlled multi-document opinion summarization. In: Proceedings of the 16th Conference of the European Chapter of the Association for Computational Linguistics: Main Volume, pp. 1646–1662. Association for Computational Linguistics, Online, April 2021. https://doi.org/10.18653/v1/2021.eacl-main.141
23. Erkan, G., Radev, D.R.: LexRank: graph-based lexical centrality as salience in text summarization. J. Artif. Intell. Res. **22**, 457–479 (2004). https://doi.org/10.1613/jair.1523
24. Friedl, K., et al.: Uncertainty aware review hallucination for science article classification. In: Zong, C., Xia, F., Li, W., Navigli, R. (eds.) Findings of the Association for Computational Linguistics: ACL/IJCNLP 2021, Online Event, 1–6 August 2021. Findings of ACL, ACL/IJCNLP 2021, pp. 5004–5009. Association for Computational Linguistics (2021). https://doi.org/10.18653/v1/2021.findings-acl.443

25. Fu, J., Ng, S., Jiang, Z., Liu, P.: GPTScore: evaluate as you desire. CoRR abs/2302.04166 (2023). https://doi.org/10.48550/arXiv.2302.04166
26. Gao, M., Ruan, J., Sun, R., Yin, X., Yang, S., Wan, X.: Human-like summarization evaluation with ChatGPT. CoRR abs/2304.02554 (2023). https://doi.org/10.48550/ARXIV.2304.02554
27. Goyal, T., Li, J.J., Durrett, G.: News summarization and evaluation in the era of GPT-3. CoRR abs/2209.12356 (2022). https://doi.org/10.48550/arXiv.2209.12356
28. Gu, N., Ash, E., Hahnloser, R.: MemSum: extractive summarization of long documents using multi-step episodic Markov decision processes. In: Proceedings of the 60th Annual Meeting of the Association for Computational Linguistics (Volume 1: Long Papers), pp. 6507–6522. Association for Computational Linguistics, Dublin, Ireland, May 2022. https://doi.org/10.18653/v1/2022.acl-long.450. https://aclanthology.org/2022.acl-long.450
29. Hu, M., Liu, B.: Opinion extraction and summarization on the web. In: Proceedings, The Twenty-First National Conference on Artificial Intelligence and the Eighteenth Innovative Applications of Artificial Intelligence Conference, 16–20 July 2006, Boston, Massachusetts, USA, pp. 1621–1624. AAAI Press (2006). http://www.aaai.org/Library/AAAI/2006/aaai06-265.php
30. Hu, Z., Chan, H.P., Yin, Y.: AMERICANO: argument generation with discourse-driven decomposition and agent interaction. CoRR abs/2310.20352 (2023). https://doi.org/10.48550/ARXIV.2310.20352
31. Iso, H., Wang, X., Suhara, Y., Angelidis, S., Tan, W.: Convex aggregation for opinion summarization. CoRR abs/2104.01371 (2021). https://arxiv.org/abs/2104.01371
32. Isonuma, M., Mori, J., Bollegala, D., Sakata, I.: Unsupervised abstractive opinion summarization by generating sentences with tree-structured topic guidance. Trans. Assoc. Comput. Linguist. **9**, 945–961 (2021). https://doi.org/10.1162/tacl_a_00406
33. Kryscinski, W., McCann, B., Xiong, C., Socher, R.: Evaluating the factual consistency of abstractive text summarization. CoRR abs/1910.12840 (2019). http://arxiv.org/abs/1910.12840
34. Kumar, A., Ghosal, T., Ekbal, A.: A deep neural architecture for decision-aware meta-review generation. In: Downie, J.S., McKay, D., Suleman, H., Nichols, D.M., Poursardar, F. (eds.) ACM/IEEE Joint Conference on Digital Libraries, JCDL 2021, Champaign, IL, USA, 27–30 September 2021, pp. 222–225. IEEE (2021). https://doi.org/10.1109/JCDL52503.2021.00064
35. Laban, P., Schnabel, T., Bennett, P.N., Hearst, M.A.: SummaC: re-visiting NLI-based models for inconsistency detection in summarization. CoRR abs/2111.09525 (2021). https://arxiv.org/abs/2111.09525
36. Li, P., Wang, Z., Ren, Z., Bing, L., Lam, W.: Neural rating regression with abstractive tips generation for recommendation. In: Kando, N., Sakai, T., Joho, H., Li, H., de Vries, A.P., White, R.W. (eds.) Proceedings of the 40th International ACM SIGIR Conference on Research and Development in Information Retrieval, Shinjuku, Tokyo, Japan, 7–11 August 2017, pp. 345–354. ACM (2017). https://doi.org/10.1145/3077136.3080822
37. Lin, C.Y.: ROUGE: a package for automatic evaluation of summaries. In: Text Summarization Branches Out, pp. 74–81. Association for Computational Linguistics, Barcelona, Spain, July 2004. https://aclanthology.org/W04-1013
38. Liu, Y., Iter, D., Xu, Y., Wang, S., Xu, R., Zhu, C.: G-eval: NLG evaluation using GPT-4 with better human alignment. CoRR abs/2303.16634 (2023). https://doi.org/10.48550/arXiv.2303.16634

39. Madaan, A., et al.: Self-refine: iterative refinement with self-feedback (2023)
40. OpenAI: ChatGPT-3.5-turbo (2021). https://openai.com/research/. Accessed 20 May 2023
41. Shen, C., Cheng, L., Zhou, R., Bing, L., You, Y., Si, L.: MReD: a meta-review dataset for structure-controllable text generation. In: Muresan, S., Nakov, P., Villavicencio, A. (eds.) Findings of the Association for Computational Linguistics: ACL 2022, Dublin, Ireland, 22–27 May 2022, pp. 2521–2535. Association for Computational Linguistics (2022). https://doi.org/10.18653/v1/2022.findings-acl.198
42. Shen, M., et al.: Simple yet effective synthetic dataset construction for unsupervised opinion summarization. CoRR abs/2303.11660 (2023). https://doi.org/10.48550/arXiv.2303.11660
43. Suhara, Y., Wang, X., Angelidis, S., Tan, W.: OpinionDigest: a simple framework for opinion summarization. In: Jurafsky, D., Chai, J., Schluter, N., Tetreault, J.R. (eds.) Proceedings of the 58th Annual Meeting of the Association for Computational Linguistics, ACL 2020, Online, 5–10 July 2020, pp. 5789–5798. Association for Computational Linguistics (2020). https://doi.org/10.18653/v1/2020.acl-main.513
44. Wang, L., Ling, W.: Neural network-based abstract generation for opinions and arguments. In: Knight, K., Nenkova, A., Rambow, O. (eds.) NAACL HLT 2016, The 2016 Conference of the North American Chapter of the Association for Computational Linguistics: Human Language Technologies, San Diego California, USA, 12–17 June 2016, pp. 47–57. The Association for Computational Linguistics (2016). https://doi.org/10.18653/v1/n16-1007
45. Wang, Q., Zeng, Q., Huang, L., Knight, K., Ji, H., Rajani, N.F.: ReviewRobot: explainable paper review generation based on knowledge synthesis. In: Davis, B., Graham, Y., Kelleher, J.D., Sripada, Y. (eds.) Proceedings of the 13th International Conference on Natural Language Generation, INLG 2020, Dublin, Ireland, 15–18 December 2020, pp. 384–397. Association for Computational Linguistics (2020). https://aclanthology.org/2020.inlg-1.44/
46. Xiao, W., Carenini, G.: Systematically exploring redundancy reduction in summarizing long documents. In: Wong, K., Knight, K., Wu, H. (eds.) Proceedings of the 1st Conference of the Asia-Pacific Chapter of the Association for Computational Linguistics and the 10th International Joint Conference on Natural Language Processing, AACL/IJCNLP 2020, Suzhou, China, 4–7 December 2020, pp. 516–528. Association for Computational Linguistics (2020). https://aclanthology.org/2020.aacl-main.51/
47. Zhang, T., Kishore, V., Wu, F., Weinberger, K.Q., Artzi, Y.: BERTScore: evaluating text generation with BERT. In: 8th International Conference on Learning Representations, ICLR 2020, Addis Ababa, Ethiopia, 26–30 April 2020. OpenReview.net (2020). https://openreview.net/forum?id=SkeHuCVFDr
48. Zhao, W., Strube, M., Eger, S.: DiscoScore: evaluating text generation with BERT and discourse coherence. CoRR abs/2201.11176 (2022). https://arxiv.org/abs/2201.11176

Curriculum Reinforcement Learning for Tokamak Control

Samy Kerboua-Benlarbi[1,2(✉)], Rémy Nouailletas[1], Blaise Faugeras[2,3], and Philippe Moreau[1]

[1] Institute for Magnetic Fusion Research - CEA, 13115 Saint-Paul-lez-Durance, France
samy.kerboua-benlarbi@cea.fr
[2] Jean Alexandre Dieudonné Laboratory - UCA, 06108 Nice, France
[3] Control, Analysis and Simulations for TOkamak Research - INRIA, 06902 Sophia Antipolis, France

Abstract. Tokamaks are the leading candidates to achieve nuclear fusion as a sustainable source of energy, and plasma control plays a crucial role in their operations. However, the complex behavior of plasma dynamics makes control of these devices challenging through traditional methods. Recent works proved the usefulness of reinforcement learning as an efficient alternative, in order to fulfill these high-dimensional and non-linear situations. Despite their performance, controlling relevant plasma configurations requires expensive and long training sessions on simulations. In this work, we leverage the use of a curriculum strategy to achieve significant speed-up in learning a controller for the control coils, which tracks plasma quantities such as shape, position and current. To this end, we developed a fast, asynchronous and reliable framework to enable interactions between a distributed actor-critic and a C++ code simulating the WEST tokamak. By sequentially increasing task complexity, results show a clear reduction in convergence time and training cost. This work is one of the first attempts to enable fast production of robust magnetic controllers, for routine use in the operations of a magnetically confined fusion device.

Keywords: Reinforcement learning · Plasma control · Neural networks

1 Introduction

Mastering nuclear fusion could significantly impact the world, unlocking the path towards sustainable and attractive means of energy production. With no direct high-level byproducts of the reaction, it has many advantages over conventional energy sources [4]. To harness this potential alternative, tokamaks are promising devices to maintain the stability and performance of plasma's confinement, despite numerous physical and control challenges [31].

Tokamaks are torus-shaped devices which aim at sustaining fusion reactions within a plasma, under specific temperature and density conditions [48]. They

W. Yin et al. (Eds.): IJCAI 2024, LNAI 14917, pp. 39–56, 2025.
https://doi.org/10.1007/978-981-97-9536-9_3

rely on magnetic fields generated by both *toroidal* and *poloidal* field (PF) coils to shape it. Interactions occur at different levels with complex dynamics involved between the plasma and its surroundings. Control systems are then required to adjust the voltages applied to the PF coils (Fig. 2), allowing control of quantities intrinsically linked to plasma's evolution, like position of the magnetic center m, *Last Closed Flux Surface* (LCFS), elongation κ and current I_p (Fig. 1). It is worth noticing that such control traditionally relies on an axisymmetry assumption for magnetic equilibria calculations, hence the cross-section representation used in this work. To study the effects of various plasma configurations, scientists rely on real-time linear controllers [34], which require substantial engineering effort whenever target scenarios undergo variations. Hence, there is an essential need for flexibility, adaptability and robustness of magnetic control systems through the entirety of the device lifetime, without which no sustained plasma could be produced.

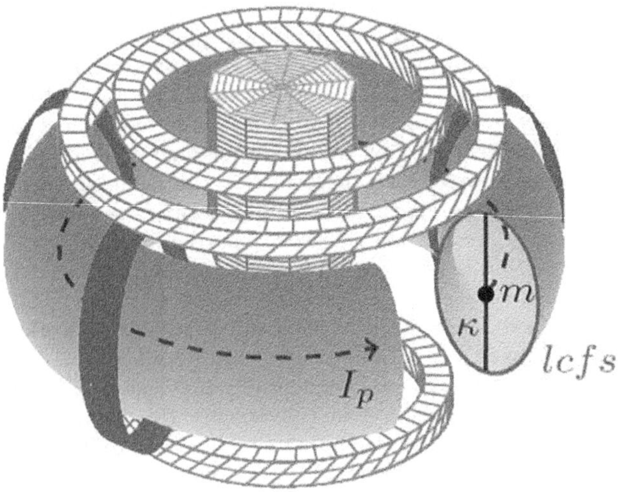

Fig. 1. Controlled quantities with toroidal (red) and poloidal (strided gold) coils. (Color figure online)

Reinforcement Learning (RL) [44] emerged as an innovative approach to numerous real-time control problems. Despite impressive results in a variety of domains [7,20,27], it usually relies on either fast and precise simulation enabling the collection of vast amount of experiences, or on direct sampling from a physical device. Both cases can not be fulfilled in our context: sampling of experimental data on the plant for the sole purpose of training is impractical, and simulations remain expensive in order to account for the coupled behavior of plasma dynamics. Despite the existence of distributed architectures as powerful tools to compensate for these bottlenecks, training still remains long and costly as the number of parallel environments increases.

In this work, we study the effects of a curriculum strategy on learning a magnetic controller through a distributed reinforcement learning framework. By improving training speed and performance, we intend to accelerate the production of robust magnetic controllers for the operation of WEST, a supraconductive tokamak located at CEA Cadarache[1] in Saint-Paul-lez-Durance, France [6,8]. Indeed, such methodology could assist plasma researchers in quickly obtaining controllers, or adapt existing ones, for each new experimental campaign, hence improving flexibility and adaptability of RL-based magnetic control.

Next sections will be organized as follows. First, we will give an overview of the related work regarding RL for tokamaks, and curriculum strategies in RL. We will then describe the curriculum methodology within plasma magnetic control, and the overall training framework. Finally, experiments are discussed through analysis of the learning dynamics. The latter will be compared to a baseline agent obtained without the strategies of interest. Finally, we will conclude on this study and its perspectives.

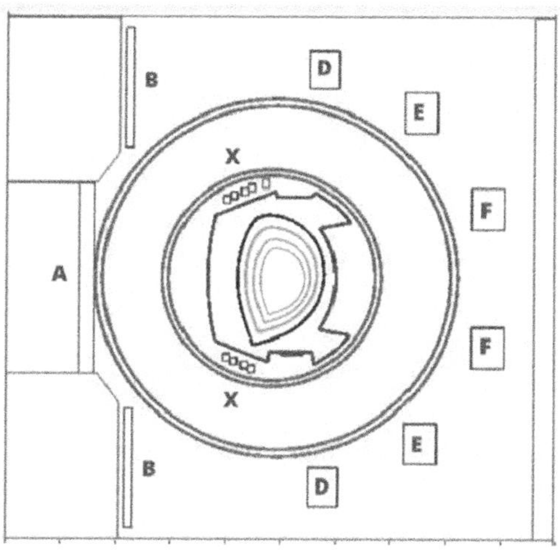

Fig. 2. Cross-section with surrounding control coils, namely poloidal field coils.

2 Background

2.1 Reinforcement Learning for Tokamaks

A classical RL framework sets an agent which interacts with an environment formalized as a *Markov Decision Process (MDP)* denoted $\mathcal{M}$. This MDP is defined by a state space $\mathcal{S}$, an action space $\mathcal{A}$, its state transition distribution

[1] French Alternative Energies and Atomic Energy Commission.

$P(s'|s,a) : \mathcal{S} \times \mathcal{A} \times \mathcal{S} \to [0,1]$, an initial state distribution $P^0(s) : \mathcal{S} \to [0,1]$, and a reward signal $R(s,a) : \mathcal{S} \times \mathcal{A} \to \mathbb{R}$.

Starting from state $s_0 \sim P^0(.)$, the agent must learn an optimal policy $\pi^* : \mathcal{S} \times \mathcal{A} \to [0,1]$, which maximizes the discounted cumulative reward, or *return*, over the course of an episode, i.e. a trajectory over states and actions from the interactions with the environment:

$$\pi^* = \underset{\pi_\theta}{\operatorname{argmax}}\, \mathbb{E}_{(s_0,a_0,\ldots,s_t,a_t)}[\sum_{k=0}^{\infty} \gamma^k r_k]$$

with discount factor $\gamma \in [0,1]$ working as a penalization term for long-term rewards, and $r_t = R(s,a) = \mathbb{E}[r_{t+1}|s_t = s, a_t = a]$. Most importantly, the reward function is a scalar feedback signal which indicates how well the agent performs with respect to the overall objectives, hence the importance of its design. The feedback loop between the agent and the environment ends once a terminal condition is reached, like a situation that we want to avoid, or a threshold on simulated time. As a side note, the policy can be deterministic, assigning a probability of 1 to the same action for each observed state. Moreover, it can be a parametrized function, like a neural network. In such cases, it is usually denoted by π_θ, where θ are the weights of the said model. Fundamental definitions arise with the value function, and the action-value function:

$$V_{\pi_\theta}(s) = \mathbb{E}_{\pi_\theta}[\sum_{k=0}^{\infty} \gamma^k r_{t+k}|s_t = s]$$

$$Q_{\pi_\theta}(s,a) = \mathbb{E}_{\pi_\theta}[\sum_{k=0}^{\infty} \gamma^k r_{t+k}|s_t = s, a_t = a]$$

It is worth mentioning that relying on the first is difficult in real-world applications such as fusion, since they do not exhibit proper knowledge of the probability transition function P. Because of that, making actions explicit is an interesting way of computing the expected return, as state-action pairs can be easily sampled throughout learning. Over the past years, the use of neural networks (NN) as powerful action-value and policy approximators lead to major advancements in continuous control problems. Deep RL algorithms such as ones from the actor-critic family kept increasing in efficiency, leading to precise control in several high-dimensional and non-linear control problems [18], both in on-policy [32,38,39] and off-policy settings [15,19,29].

Consequently, deep reinforcement learning is becoming increasingly popular among the plasma control community. For example, RL has been used for model-based control [10], for vertical stabilization [11,13], to build feedforward trajectories of plasma parameters [41], for temperature and profile control [46,47], or even for tearing instability control and disruption avoidance [40]. Recent works [12] designed a RL-based system which achieved magnetic control of the *Tokamak à Configuration Variable* (TCV), in Lausanne, Switzerland. The learned controller demonstrates the capability for RL-based systems to tackle various complex plasma configurations while tracking many quantities of interest at the same time. A similar procedure was proposed by [26], with the same limitations of the initial proposal, while refining the simulation on which magnetic controllers were trained.

These examples highlight a shift of focus from classical controllers, designed using prior knowledge on how control should be performed with respect to physical properties of the dynamical system, to controllers learning by trial-and-error to act on the system based on what should be achieved in terms of final objectives. In summary, deep RL advantages over classical tokamak control stem from its ability to: fulfill these high dimensional, uncertain and non-linear systems; explore possible strategies in order to make the control policy more flexible in contrast with the fixed heuristics of classical control; learn from raw magnetic signals using neural networks, since plasma quantities can not be measured directly, and are instead usually inferred in real-time from reconstruction codes [9,14] for use by classical controllers.

2.2 Curriculum Learning for Reinforcement Learning

Curriculum learning (CL) [5] is a methodology to optimize the order in which experiences are processed by an agent over the course of training. From the early stages of human development to adulthood, learning is structured and organized sequentially, so that the knowledge acquired over time facilitates the understanding of new notions or tasks that occur later to us. Therefore, a sequence of increasingly difficult tasks implicitly builds a curriculum, as knowledge is transferred from one intermediate objective to the other. Scheduling and designing such strategy helps in acquiring transferable skills to guide exploration during training, with the premise of increased performance and reduced convergence time towards a final set of tasks. Recent works classified the taxonomy of existing methods [42] as well as a formal framework for curriculum learning in reinforcement learning domains using graphs [33]. In most cases, we consider different MDPs between each task and three main concepts arise with which CL methods can be classified: the intermediate task generation, the partial ordering on the obtained set of tasks, and how knowledge could be shared between its elements. Considering the importance of human intuition to define simple tasks [5], domain experts could efficiently make a distinction between objectives that are neither "too easy" or "too hard". Indeed, task generation and sequencing of the latter could be handcrafted from human operators [30,43], but both concepts could be built up automatically as part of the curriculum learning procedure [17,24,50]. Transfer learning methods are required to share knowledge representation at each step of the curriculum, and concern several elements of the training loop, such as entire policies and value functions, rewards, etc. [51]. Care must be taken while choosing the right combinations of methods, to avoid negative transfer which could harm controllers performance [49].

3 Approach

3.1 Motivation

RL is still an emerging field within plasma magnetic control, and few applications are observable. It can take several days of training for control efficiency on relative simple plasma scenarios [12,26]. Nevertheless, the routine operation of a tokamak requires flexibility over the design of controllers. Minimum engineering efforts should be targeted to adapt and fine-tune the controllers with respect to the objectives of each new experimental campaign.

For this reason, this study aims at assessing the effects of CL in the context of tokamak control, where poor reward signal and state representation at the beginning of learning, can destabilize the whole training process. We do not specifically intend to reach a new general performance threshold, but look for increased performance at start of each new task, specializing exploration as training evolves towards its final goal. Considering the cost of data sampling using WEST simulations, yet in the real world, curriculum learning could be of great help to stabilize the entire procedure, and reduce convergence time by several orders of magnitude. Furthermore, each new experimental campaign on WEST requires the definition of multiple control scenarios. The latter might have shared plasma states, and overall control objectives. This means that the same events can be used within different scenarios, especially while choosing initial conditions or terminal ones. Since a scenario is a sequence of events, their ordering already defines a curriculum in an implicit manner, as plasma equilibriums must follow each other in a realistic and feasible way. Moreover, one could go further by explicitly building a curriculum on the reward function, considering a sequence on its definition, i.e. directly on the explicit control objective which might be similar between scenarios. A simple reward on the shape for example could be used as a starter, latter including the elongation, etc. Both ideas lead to the same conclusion regarding CL in fusion:

- curriculum generation and ordering could describe tasks as events, or intermediate reward definitions;
- the two approaches shows that a curriculum working for one plasma scenario, could be intuitively generalizable with little effort on similar ones, enhancing production of controllers for several cases during experimental campaigns.

It is worth noticing that [45] addressed the initial drawbacks of the method described by [12], i.e. training speed and steady-state performance of the controller. Their approach resembles curriculum learning by borrowing its codes. Researchers partition a target scenario in smaller chunks, each related to one part of the general task. Distributed environments are then divided into subsests of different cardinalities, each linked to one of the said chunks. Experiences are accumulated from MDPs that differs implicitly in their underlying dynamics. Sampled experiences are more diverse, and mix multiple levels of difficulty inside the same training procedure. This approach already reduced training time by a factor of 4. However, despite different initial state distributions, the overall task remains the same between chunks, and no proper curriculum is defined, i.e. no knowledge transfer is present and task ordering is not specifically mentioned. An interesting outcome shows that the two methods can be combined. This is done by splitting the scenario in chunks, and all of them would then sequentially refer to the same task definition. In the following sections, we will consider the combined procedure in order to benefit from both approaches.

3.2 Curriculum Definition

Formalism. Let τ be a set of tasks with $m_i : (\mathcal{S}, \mathcal{A}, P_i, R_i) \in \tau$, all sharing the same state and action spaces. Moreover, we denote $\mathcal{D}^\tau$, the set of all transitions belonging to τ, so that $\mathcal{D}^\tau = \{(s, a, r, s') \mid \exists\, m_i \in \tau, s \in \mathcal{S}, a \in \mathcal{A}, s' \sim P_i(.|s,a), r = R_i(s,a)\}$. A curriculum $\mathcal{C}$ can then be defined as a direct acyclic graph ($\mathcal{V}$, ε, H, τ), with $\mathcal{V}$ vertices, ε edges, $H : \mathcal{V} \to \mathcal{P}(\mathcal{D}^\tau)$, connecting $v \in \mathcal{V}$ to a subset of samples of $\mathcal{D}^\tau$. An edge $< v_j, v_k >$ of $\mathcal{C}$ links two tasks, using all samples associated by H to v_j before transferring to v_k. For each $m_i \in \tau$, we have $\mathcal{D}_i^\tau = \{(s, a, r, s') \mid s \in \mathcal{S}_i = \mathcal{S}, a \in \mathcal{A}_i = \mathcal{A}, s' \sim P_i(.|s,a), r = R_i(s,a)\}$. We need to associate all $v \in \mathcal{V}$ with corresponding m_i and $\mathcal{D}_i^\tau$, meaning that each path on the graph directly influences how $H : \mathcal{V} \to \{\mathcal{D}_i^\tau | m_i \in \tau\}$ filters knowledge transfer between tasks, with edges built on properties of the samples associated with successive nodes. Indeed, tasks must be ordered properly so that π_i^* is useful for acquiring good samples at each transition on the current vertex. In our case, a task is associated with only one vertex, and each intermediate vertex sinks in only one node until the final one is reached, i.e. the final task [33]. This defines an oriented sequence of tasks, similar to what was previously stated in terms of curriculum learning.

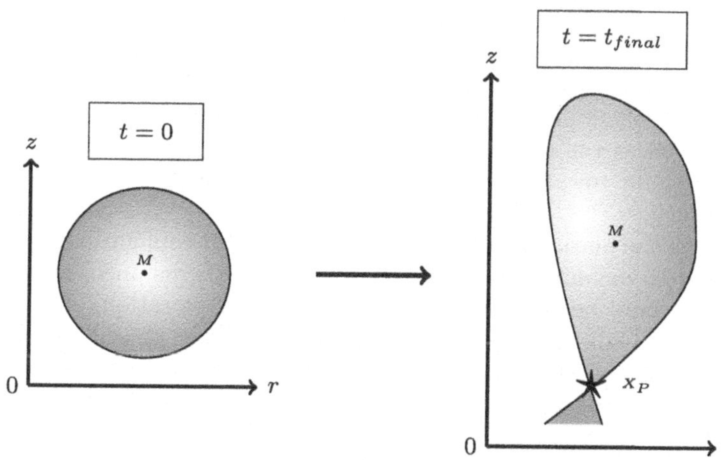

Fig. 3. Schematic view of the scenario of interest. It starts from a limiter configuration, and ends up by stabilizing an elongated plasma with an X-point (X_P) represented as a star.

Tasks. In this work, tasks are defined on the reward function, and only one scenario is considered for learning a controller. We focus on transitioning from a "circular" shaped plasma in limiter configuration, to an elongated plasma in X-point (X_p) configuration, i.e. $\kappa > 1$ (Fig. 3). A plasma can be seen as a succession of nested closed magnetic flux surfaces. The *Last Closed Flux Surface* (LCFS) defines the plasma boundary, which evolves until reaching the desired configuration. Once the latter is achieved, the LCFS is surrounded by open surfaces, while the X-point appears at its intersection. Specifically, elongated configurations have improved confinement properties compared to limiter plasmas, at the cost of developing growing vertical instabilities which make control more difficult. The chosen curriculum is entirely conditioned by a set of predefined rewards R_i. This means that while it could have been defined automatically, the uncertainty around tokamak dynamics makes the choice for a handcrafted sequence of tasks quite straightforward for this first application. Prior control experience on the device informs on which tasks could be considered easier than others. This work then relies on human experts for both determining $\mathcal{T}$, as well as the resulting sequence order based on $\mathcal{V}$ and ε. More precisely, the curriculum has been built from physical intuition around several key control challenges studied for all tokamaks (Fig. 4):

1. vertical stabilization of elongated plasmas while tracking plasma current is a well-known control problem. Using classical feedback control, simple proportional-integral-derivative (PID) controllers [3] can stabilize plasma's magnetic center (r_m, z_m), as well as plasma current I_p. Their relative simplicity is not far from a basic RL-based solution, as a naive agent could be summarized as proportional-integral control which reduces errors between observations and targets. The initial reward function then includes targets for the two elements of interest. Hence, handling such classical problem is a good start in order to build strong foundations for the next tasks;
2. tracking the entire plasma boundary becomes more challenging, as approaches from classical control often relies on more advanced methods to synthesize efficient controllers. Since the difficulty becomes more important, we add the LCFS as well as the elongation to the initial targets. This creates a way to guide the agent towards an elongated shape, properly positioning it before the final task;
3. finally, once the plasma is set up towards its X-point configuration, we modify the reward to include targets on the X-point itself (distance, magnetic flux, etc.). This could be considered as a fine-tuning exploration, since the agent must have already positioned the plasma boundary according to the final configuration. Nevertheless, we must proceed with caution, in order to avoid loosing accuracy on previous tasks through catastrophic forgetting [16].

Transfer Learning. We transfer the policy and the action-value function between tasks, with both of them represented by neural networks. The parameters of $\mathcal{Q}_i$ learned during an intermediate task, serves as initialization for the parameters of

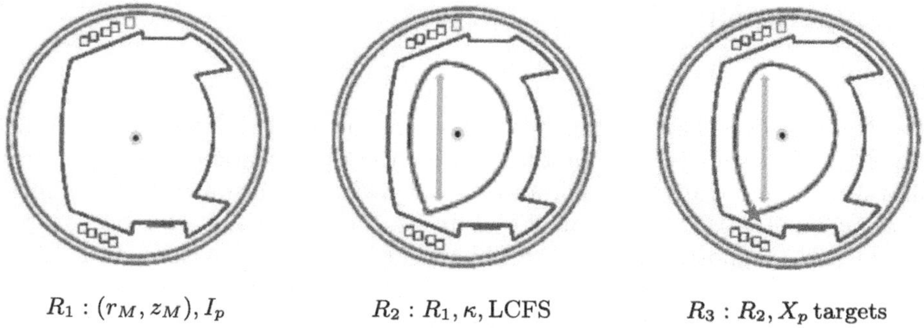

Fig. 4. Curriculum overview. We start from a simple vertical control stabilization problem with an evolving plasma current, to a complex one involving shape and X-point.

the next action-value function Q_j, without any freezing procedure which could negatively impact transfer [49]. Doing so bias the agent towards more efficient exploration in the next domain. The policy's weights are also used to initialize the parameters of the new one, again without any freezing procedure. One could have incrementally frozen layers between tasks in order to keep previous representations learned by the controller. However, we empirically observed that it is not necessary for the curriculum learning to work well in practice. Furthermore, it limits the amount of tasks present in the curriculum, as the number of layers is bounded. We further use *potential-based advice* reward shaping (PBARS) so that $R'_j(s,a) = R_i(s,a) + F(s,a) + R_j(s,a)$ with $F(s,a,s',a') = Q_i(s',a') - Q_i(s,a)$. R_i retains knowledge from the source task and F encourages exploration from states that were valuable and overlap with the target j. They form the potential-based bonus with guarantees that it will not change the optimal policy [21].

Transfer Metrics. While final performance on the target task will be analyzed, our main objective is to observe how CL could produce RL-based magnetic controllers faster, for routine use on WEST. Metrics must be chosen accordingly in order to measure by how much it speeds up training, compared to the vanilla method where the agent learn directly on the final task. We will refer to this question with two tools: the *jumpstart* and the *Time to threshold* (TTT). The former measures the initial performance increase at the beginning of each new task as a result of transfer; the latter checks how much faster the agent learns the policy which reaches a threshold on the episode return for the final task, with or without curriculum. Each intermediate task is caped to a maximum duration of 60 evaluation episodes, mostly to stay in line with empirical observations regarding time taken by the warmup phase, i.e. the phase during which trained NNs do not undergo real variations.

4 Experiments

4.1 Setup

The NICE Code. The environment is based on the NICE C++ code [14], which solves the *Grad-Shafranov* equation [48] for the plasma domain, with resistive diffusion [22] and transport equation enabled. We use its forward evolution mode which computes the environment's state at each timestep. Moreover, power supply and diagnostic models are implemented in order to account for bias, delays and offsets of actuators. Overall, it gives an accurate representation of the plasma, as well as the WEST control system. NICE is safely initialized to a limiter shaped plasma extracted from recent experimental data, whose internal profiles are randomized to promote diversity among examples. Such randomization is performed according to a study of NICE convergence under variations of three parameters, all defining the parametric representations responsible for the said initial profiles. In this 3-dimensional parameter space, the obtained hypercube is used to sample a triplet at the beginning of each new episode, which minimizes the risk of NICE not converging. By doing so, we ensure a more representative set of examples regarding plasma evolution, while avoiding a change in the initial shape which has been specifically chosen because of its numerical stability. The relative error of the Newton solver is increased to accelerate execution without significant loose of accuracy in its outputs. Termination is triggered if thresholds are reached on active coils currents or safety factor (proportional to the geometry of the plasma and its current), to avoid any damage on the device. The simulation step size is set to 1 ms, with episodes typically lasting for 350 timesteps, as it appears long enough for transitions between the two configurations of interest on WEST.

Table 1. Reward components description with dimensions. Scaling to [0, 1] range is performed, before combination to a final scalar value. Alpha is specified for each component if it has multiple targets. Flux setpoints are set to 1 since their measure is normalized, while flux gradient must tend towards zero.

Component	Good	Bad	α	weight
LCFS [m]	0.005	0.1	-1	3.
Magnetic center [m]	0.002	0.03	x	1.
κ	0.005	0.03	x	1.
I_p [kA]	0.5	20	x	3.
X point distance [m]	0.01	0.15	x	2.
Flux at current x point	0.	1.	x	2.
Flux at target x point	0.	0.08	x	2.
Flux gradient at target x point	0.	4.	x	1.
Final combiner: *Smoothmax*($\alpha = -0.5$)				

State and Action Spaces. The environment's state is defined as $s = \{y, I_a, m\}$ with y the plasma equilibrium information, I_a the currents in the active control coils, and m the raw magnetic measurements. y typically contains all quantities of interest described in the curriculum definition. It is usually difficult to observe the entirety of s in real-time. To overcome this issue, the learned policy is restricted to a *Partially Observable MDP* (POMDP) where the state space is limited to the observation space $\mathcal{O}$. As such, we have $o(s) = \{tr, m_b, fl, I_a, \frac{dm_b}{dt}\}$, with tr target references, $\{m_b, fl\}$ magnetic probes and flux loops raw measurements, and $\frac{dm_b}{dt}$, temporal derivatives of magnetic probes signals. Noise is injected in observations at each timestep from Gaussian laws with parameters identified from WEST plasma discharges database, as well as delays to model real data acquisition from sensors. For actions, voltages are sampled from Gaussian distributions which parameters are the outputs of the control policy, and then supplied to each of the 11 PFCs circumventing the device (Fig. 1 - Naming conventions stated in Fig. 2). After exploring possible outcomes during training, only the mean of each distribution is kept at inference to predict optimal actions. Offsets, bias and delays are part of the power supply model within NICE to ensure correct handling of WEST actuators in the real world.

Rewards. Each reward R_i is a normalized weighted combination of error signals, extended with PBARS. Each component c_i^j is computed as the difference E_j between its target value and the one retrieved from the environment, then scaled to $[0, 1]$ with $Softplus(E_j) := min(max(2 \cdot \sigma(-log(19)(\frac{E_j - good}{bad - good})), 0), 1)$. They are then combined into a final scalar within the same interval using the function $Smoothmax(\alpha, R_i, W) := \sum_j w_j R_i^j e^{\alpha R_i^j} / \sum_j w_j e^{\alpha R_i^j}$. If one component is made out of several targets, an intermediate combination using the latter is also performed. *Good* and *bad* parameters in the *Softplus* formulation, scale the reward signal according to regions of interest in the reward space. Tight values in both parameters will lead to higher focus on the component to achieve high reward. Smoother values will help exploration at the cost of precise control. Weights in the *Smoothmax* definition affect the importance of each reward component, while the α defines focus balance between them. Specifically, we combine all 32 distances between computed and reference points of the LCFS with $w = 1$ and $\alpha = -1$. Reward undergo a final scaling, so that the maximum cumulative reward for 350 ms equals 35. For a description of each component's weight and parameters, please refer to Table 1.

Agent. In this work, a distributed *Maximum à Posteriori Policy Optimization* (MPO) [1,2] is used, which have shown strong empirical results on a wide range of control problems, including fusion. It is part of a recent interpretation of RL as probabilistic inference [28]. Since our environment is computationally expensive, such paradigm is useful to reach faster convergence compared to a variety of policy gradient methods, while avoiding the use of on-policy algorithm such as *Proximal Policy Optimization* (PPO) [39]. Our implementation is distributed, and composed of 95 multi-layered perceptrons (MLP) for the actors, and a Long-Short-Term-Memory (LSTM) for the critic [23]. MLPs help the first to stay fast

Table 2. Agent's hyperparameters.

Hyperparameter	Chosen value
Batch size	256
Discount factor	0.99
Sequence length for critic	64
Burn-in length critic	10
π_σ	0.5
ϵ	0.5
ϵ_μ	9.09e−5
ϵ_σ	9.09e−8
learning rate	3e−4
dual learning rate	1e−2

enough for real-time control constraints in case of deployment on the real device; the LSTM allows the second to better represent interaction dynamics through longer sequences. Moreover, this asymmetric setup has been shown to be more efficient than one solely relying on MLPs [12]. As stated previously, we use stochastic policies which predict a mean and a standard deviation for each of the 11 control coils. Once training is completed, exploring possible outcomes is not needed anymore. As a consequence, only the mean of each distribution is kept at inference to predict optimal actions. Sequences are partitioned so that a *burn-in* phase takes place at each learning step, i.e. part of each input sequence sampled from the replay buffer is used to initialize the LSTM core [25]. Adam optimizer is used both for the critic and the actor networks. Specific hyperparameters chosen for NNs definition can be found in Table 2, while others follow previous works. They either come from a grid search, kept narrow to evade an explosion of the computational budget, or directly reused as is from [26].

Training Framework. The interaction loop can be described as follows: a learner worker uses information gathered within a replay buffer to optimize policy and critic NNs; actor threads work independently from each other. Each thread spans a UDS protocol client-server interface with its own random seed, in which the policy interacts with an instance of NICE, sending data to the replay buffer asynchronously; each actor updates its control policy by copying weights periodically from the learner. Evaluation is performed on a separate thread during training for monitoring purposes, using only the mean of the current policy as stated before. This results in a fast and reliable, multi-threaded and multi-GPU framework, running numerous instances of the NICE environment in parallel to learn a control policy in Python (Fig. 5). Policy networks are all restricted to CPU, in order to lower simulation to reality gaps. Every aspect of the framework then ensures that training can put the agent in realistic conditions with regards to the machine's usual operation. Experiments are performed on a NVIDIA®

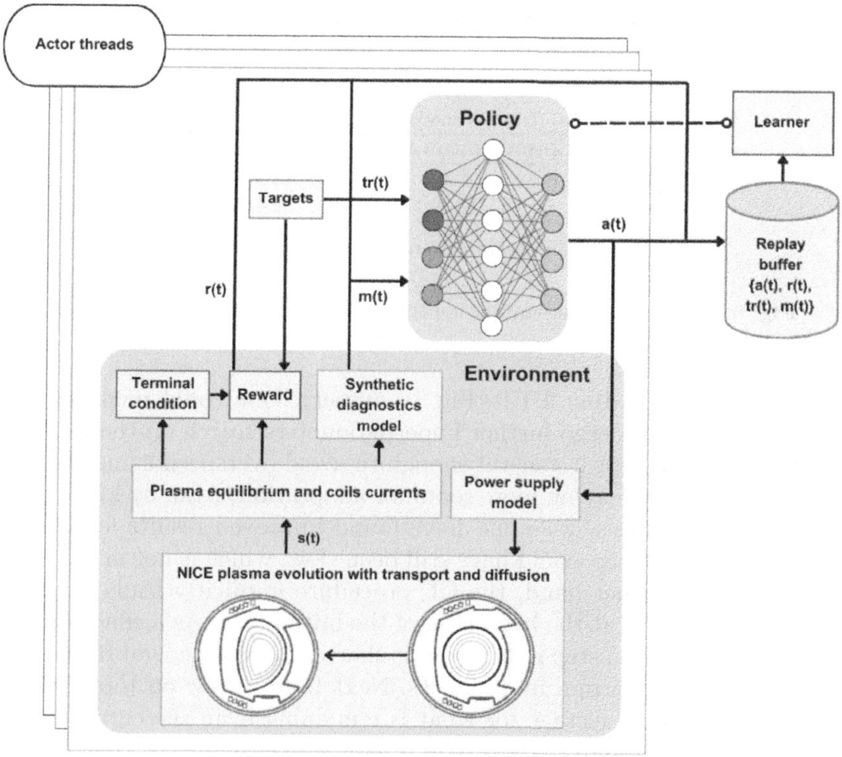

Fig. 5. Framework's overview.

Tesla™ V100S for the learner, and Intel® Cascade Lake® 6248 at 2.50 GHz for the C++ environments. As a side note, the framework is flexible enough to allow fast update or addition of new control scenarios.

4.2 Results

Training results are averaged over 3 different seeds of the evaluator thread. The reward threshold for the TTT is set to 25, as control starts to perform relatively well in such conditions.

Firstly, we know that an environment's step within NICE lasts for about 13 s on average during exploration, since the plasma reaches locations of the vacuum chamber in which convergence of the simulation is more difficult. This means that in the complex case, where poor reward signals are common, exploration is long and tedious, increasing computing time of an episode up to almost 2 h if the latter reaches its full duration of 350 timesteps. Based on this idea, the monitored training time for the vanilla method easily reaches the symbolic threshold of an entire week. Moreover, the reward never exceeds 20 inside the 60 episodes cap scope, and struggles to reach 25 afterwards, which is way under

Method	Jumpstart on the final task	TTT
Vanilla	4.3	180h
CL	-10.2	60h

(a) Transfer metrics across seeds.

	Episode mean reward	Error margin
Vanilla	5.2	±3.65
CL	18.4	±4.23

(b) Mean reward over tasks and across seeds.

Fig. 6. Analysis of the vanilla control policy against the CL method.

our expectations regarding TTT (Fig. 7 - upper). One could mention the fact that we could have undergo further hyperparameters search on the reward definition. However, we kept it general enough to avoid overspecializing the method towards one scenario, leaving more room for adaptation. Also, by looking at better reward specifications, we could have found improved results for the vanilla method, but convergence would have still been slow, which is not in line with our main goal. On the other hand, the CL procedure implicitly leads to reachable states that are "easier" at the beginning of the initial task. As a consequence, the duration of a simulation step in this case is shorter in average, and the simulation converges to an equilibrium in about 2 s. Next tasks follow on top of this idea, which leads to 8.7 s in average for what is remaining from the curriculum. This leads to episodes computed at worst in a little more than 1 h for complex tasks if the maximum episode duration is reached, which is already an interesting outcome. With that in mind, the reward threshold is reached in about 120 episodes, and the TTT is reduced to approximately 60 h. As a matter of fact, we observe a clear reduction in convergence time towards the reward threshold, sufficient to gain proper control of the plasma in the configuration of interest (Fig. 6a). We stopped training before 60 evaluation episodes for the final task, since the return was stable and close to 25. If we look at the jumpstart using the total number of episodes, CL actually performs equally, if not worse, than the best obtained return for the vanilla method at each curriculum step (Fig. 7 - upper). A simple explanation comes from the fact that the added reward complexity inevitably drops the initial return. Another explanation could arise from catastrophic forgetting, but a more rigorous evaluation is required to confirm this hypothesis. After those sudden drops, the agent fails its first attempt, especially on the last task, but ends up recovering. Let us recall that we are not stopping previous tasks based on performance, but rather constraining the entire training time to 60 evaluation episodes. So, this situation is not entirely surprising, since no optimal behavior is guaranteed at the end of each intermediate curriculum step. Moreover, MPO requires several initial exploratory episodes, in order for training to start concretely. This means that the overall method could also be analyzed without those warm-up interactions, restricting the figure to the last 20 meaningful episodes for example (Fig. 7 - lower). In this case, both metrics gives better results, as only improved behaviors are taken into account: the jumpstart

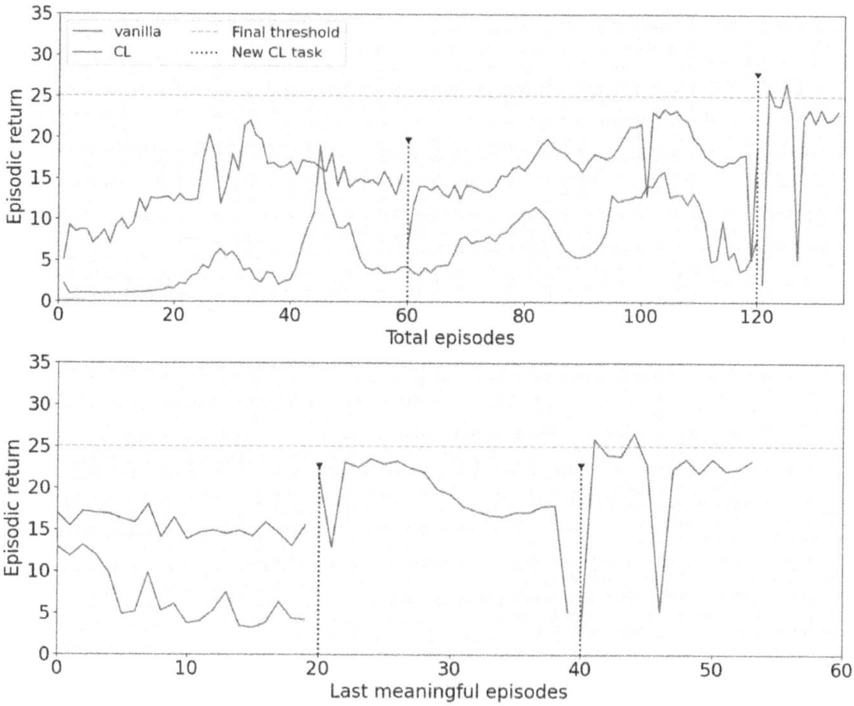

Fig. 7. Episodic return for both methods (vanilla - red, CL - green). Since MPO goes through a warm-up phase, we consider the last episodes that were meaningful regarding reward convergence. (Color figure online)

is significantly higher, despite the last drop for the last transition, and the time to threshold is even lower.

CL does clearly improve the average performance on the final task (Fig. 6b), as it performs better than the vanilla policy (Figs. 7 - both). It enhances magnetic control, showing that the method does not induce any training instabilities, apart from potential catastrophic forgetting.

5 Conclusion and Perspectives

Curriculum learning displays interesting results in terms of convergence time, while reaching higher levels of performance than a controller exhibits when trained from scratch. Through the simple definition of a sequence of tasks in terms of reward functions, robust magnetic controllers are obtained three times faster than baseline training which requires at least a week. This work is one of the first attempts along with [45] to look for practical means of speeding up training of RL-based magnetic controllers. The two methods are also not orthogonal, and combining them leads to the same conclusion.

However, we fixed the action space between tasks, but using the 11 coils might not be useful all the time. Same goes for the magnetic measurements, since nothing indicates that all sensors are always useful. Automatic sequencing of the action and state spaces definitions could help in improving the curriculum generation. Moreover, this work considers only one curriculum, applied to a single scenario of interest. Further works would benefit from more extensive evaluations and ablation studies to properly identify the effects of each component (tasks ordering, reward shaping) on the curriculum learning strategy.

A clear limitation of the method comes from the risk of catastrophic forgetting, since we transfer without freezing weights. In-depth analysis and improvement of the root causes (replay buffer [35], NN sizes, etc.) which could cause such phenomenon would help in performing better transfer of the policy between tasks. An interesting perspective lies in the use of *Progressive Neural Networks* (PNN) [37], which are not affected by catastrophic forgetting and are theoretically capable of handling complete different tasks. However, big architectures for the actors can not efficiently work on real-time control systems due to predictions slower than the timescale of many plasma events. One solution could come from *Policy Distillation* [36]. By training PNNs through curriculum learning, powerful expert policies could be obtained quickly, and distilled into a smaller network in line with our operational constraints.

Acknowledgments. This work was supported by Capgemini Engineering and the Provence Alpes Côte d'Azur region. It was granted access to the HPC resources of IDRIS under the allocation 20XX-AD010514319 made by GENCI.

Disclosure of Interests. The authors have no competing interests to declare that are relevant to the content of this article.

References

1. Abdolmaleki, A., et al.: Maximum a posteriori policy optimisation. arXiv preprint arXiv:1806.06920 (2018)
2. Abdolmaleki, A., et al.: Relative entropy regularized policy iteration. arXiv preprint arXiv:1812.02256 (2018)
3. Ang, K.H., Chong, G., Li, Y.: PID control system analysis, design, and technology. IEEE Trans. Control Syst. Technol. **13**(4), 559–576 (2005)
4. Ariola, M., Pironti, A.: Magnetic Control of Tokamak Plasmas. Springer, London (2008). https://doi.org/10.1007/978-1-84800-324-8
5. Bengio, Y., Louradour, J., Collobert, R., Weston, J.: Curriculum learning. In: Proceedings of the 26th Annual International Conference on Machine Learning, pp. 41–48. Association for Computing Machinery (2009)
6. Bourdelle, C., Artaud, J.F., et al.: West physics basis. Nucl. Fusion **55**(6), 063–017 (2015)
7. Brohan, A., Brown, N., et al.: RT-1: robotics transformer for real-world control at scale (2023)
8. Bucalossi, J., et al.: Operating a full tungsten actively cooled tokamak: overview of west first phase of operation. Nucl. Fusion **62**(4), 042007 (2022)

9. Carpanese, F.: Development of free-boundary equilibrium and transport solvers for simulation and real-time interpretation of tokamak experiments, p. 238 (2021)
10. Char, I., Abbate, J., et al.: Offline model-based reinforcement learning for tokamak control. In: Proceedings of Machine Learning Research, vol. 211, pp. 1357–1372. PMLR (2023)
11. De Tommasi, G., Dubbioso, S., et al.: A RL-based vertical stabilization system for the east tokamak. In: 2022 American Control Conference (ACC), pp. 5328–5333 (2022)
12. Degrave, J., Felici, F., et al.: Magnetic control of tokamak plasmas through deep reinforcement learning. Nature **602**(7897), 414–419 (2022)
13. Dubbioso, S., De Tommasi, G., et al.: A deep reinforcement learning approach for vertical stabilization of tokamak plasmas. Fusion Eng. Des. **194**, 113725 (2023)
14. Faugeras, B.: An overview of the numerical methods for tokamak plasma equilibrium computation implemented in the nice code. Fusion Eng. Des. **160**, 112020 (2020)
15. Fujimoto, S., Hoof, H., Meger, D.: Addressing function approximation error in actor-critic methods. In: International Conference on Machine Learning, pp. 1587–1596. PMLR (2018)
16. Goodfellow, I.J., Mirza, M., Xiao, D., Courville, A., Bengio, Y.: An empirical investigation of catastrophic forgetting in gradient-based neural networks (2015)
17. Graves, A., Bellemare, M.G., Menick, J., Munos, R., Kavukcuoglu, K.: Automated curriculum learning for neural networks (2017)
18. Grondman, I., Busoniu, L., Lopes, G.A.D., Babuska, R.: A survey of actor-critic reinforcement learning: standard and natural policy gradients. IEEE Trans. Syst. Man Cybern. Part C (Appl. Rev.) **42**(6), 1291–1307 (2012)
19. Haarnoja, T., Zhou, A., Abbeel, P., Levine, S.: Soft actor-critic: off-policy maximum entropy deep reinforcement learning with a stochastic actor. In: International Conference on Machine Learning, pp. 1861–1870. PMLR (2018)
20. Han, D., Mulyana, B., Stankovic, V., Cheng, S.: A survey on deep reinforcement learning algorithms for robotic manipulation. Sensors **23**(7) (2023)
21. Harutyunyan, A., Devlin, S., Vrancx, P., Nowe, A.: Expressing arbitrary reward functions as potential-based advice. Proc. AAAI Conf. Artif. Intell. **29**(1) (2015). https://doi.org/10.1609/aaai.v29i1.9628
22. Heumann, H.: A Galerkin method for the weak formulation of current diffusion and force balance in tokamak plasmas. J. Comput. Phys. **442** (2021)
23. Hoffman, M.W., et al.: Acme: a research framework for distributed reinforcement learning. arXiv preprint arXiv:2006.00979 (2020)
24. Ivanovic, B., Harrison, J., et al.: BaRC: backward reachability curriculum for robotic reinforcement learning. In: 2019 International Conference on Robotics and Automation (ICRA), pp. 15–21. IEEE (2019)
25. Kapturowski, S., Ostrovski, G., et al.: Recurrent experience replay in distributed reinforcement learning. In: International Conference on Learning Representations (2018)
26. Kerboua-Benlarbi, S., Nouailletas, R., Faugeras, B., Nardon, E., Moreau, P.: Magnetic control of west plasmas through deep reinforcement learning. IEEE Trans. Plasma Sci., 1–0 (2024). https://doi.org/10.1109/TPS.2024.3377811
27. Kiran, B.R., Sobh, I., et al.: Deep reinforcement learning for autonomous driving: a survey. IEEE Trans. Intell. Transp. Syst. **23**(6), 4909–4926 (2022)
28. Levine, S.: Reinforcement learning and control as probabilistic inference: tutorial and review (2018)

29. Lillicrap, T.P., Hunt, J.J., et al.: Continuous control with deep reinforcement learning. arXiv preprint arXiv:1509.02971 (2015)
30. MacAlpine, P., Stone, P.: Overlapping layered learning. Artif. Intell. **254**, 21–43 (2018)
31. Meade, D.: 50 years of fusion research. Nucl. Fusion **50**(1), 014004 (2009). https://doi.org/10.1088/0029-5515/50/1/014004
32. Mnih, V., Badia, A.P., et al.: Asynchronous methods for deep reinforcement learning. In: International Conference on Machine Learning, pp. 1928–1937. PMLR (2016)
33. Narvekar, S., Peng, B., et al.: Curriculum learning for reinforcement learning domains: a framework and survey. J. Mach. Learn. Res. **21**(1), 7382–7431 (2020)
34. Nouailletas, R., Moreau, P., et al.: West plasma control system status. Fusion Eng. Des. **192**, 113582 (2023)
35. Rolnick, D., Ahuja, A., Schwarz, J., Lillicrap, T.P., Wayne, G.: Experience replay for continual learning. CoRR abs/1811.11682 (2018)
36. Rusu, A.A., Colmenarejo, S.G., et al.: Policy distillation (2016)
37. Rusu, A.A., Rabinowitz, N.C., et al.: Progressive neural networks. CoRR abs/1606.04671 (2016). http://arxiv.org/abs/1606.04671
38. Schulman, J., Levine, S., et al.: Trust region policy optimization. In: International Conference on Machine Learning, pp. 1889–1897. PMLR (2015)
39. Schulman, J., Wolski, F., et al.: Proximal policy optimization algorithms. arXiv preprint arXiv:1707.06347 (2017)
40. Seo, J., Kim, S., Jalalvand, A., et al.: Avoiding fusion plasma tearing instability with deep reinforcement learning. Nature **626**, 746–751 (2024). https://doi.org/10.1038/s41586-024-07024-9
41. Seo, J., Na, Y.S., et al.: Feedforward beta control in the KSTAR tokamak by deep reinforcement learning. Nucl. Fusion **61**(10), 106010 (2021)
42. Soviany, P., Ionescu, R.T., Rota, P., Sebe, N.: Curriculum learning: a survey. Int. J. Comput. Vision **130**(6), 1526–1565 (2022)
43. Stanley, K.O., Bryant, B.D., Miikkulainen, R.: Evolving neural network agents in the Nero video game (2005)
44. Sutton, R.S., Barto, A.G.: Reinforcement Learning: An Introduction. MIT Press (2018)
45. Tracey, B.D., Michi, A., The TCV Team, et al.: Towards practical reinforcement learning for tokamak magnetic control. ArXiv abs/2307.11546 (2023)
46. Wakatsuki, T., Suzuki, T., et al.: Safety factor profile control with reduced central solenoid flux consumption during plasma current ramp-up phase using a reinforcement learning technique. Nucl. Fusion **59**(6), 066022 (2019)
47. Wakatsuki, T., Suzuki, T., Oyama, N., Hayashi, N.: Ion temperature gradient control using reinforcement learning technique. Nucl. Fusion **61**(4), 046036 (2021)
48. Wesson, J.: Tokamaks 3rd edition. J. Plasma Phys. **71**(3), 377 (2004). https://doi.org/10.1017/S0022377804003058
49. Wołczyk, M., Zając, M., Pascanu, R., Kuciński, Ł., Miłoś, P.: Disentangling transfer in continual reinforcement learning (2022)
50. Wu, Y., Tian, Y.: Training agent for first-person shooter game with actor-critic curriculum learning. In: International Conference on Learning Representations (2017)
51. Zhu, Z., Lin, K., Jain, A.K., Zhou, J.: Transfer learning in deep reinforcement learning: a survey. IEEE Trans. Pattern Anal. Mach. Intell. **45**(11) (2023). https://doi.org/10.1109/TPAMI.2023.3292075

AutoEncoder-Based Anomaly Detection for CMS Data Quality Monitoring

Alkis Papanastassiou[1,2,3](✉), Valentina Gori[3], Piergiulio Lenzi[1,2], and on behalf of the CMS Collaboration

[1] Universiy of Florence, Florence, Italy
alkis.papanastassiou@unifi.it
[2] Istituto Nazionale di Fisica Nucleare (INFN), Rome, Italy
[3] Baker Hughes, Houston, USA

Abstract. The monitoring of data quality in high-energy physics experiments is essential during both data acquisition and offline analyses to ensure the reliability of datasets. The Compact Muon Solenoid (CMS) experiment at the Large Hadron Collider (LHC) has recently implemented Data Quality Monitoring (DQM) at the granularity of individual "luminosity sections" (LSs), each corresponding to approximately 23 seconds of data collection. This paper presents a novel application of AutoEncoders for anomaly detection in DQM, specifically targeting quantities associated with jets and missing transverse energy (MET). The developed method allows for the detection of anomalies at the LS level, which might be missed when examining integrated quantities. By automating the identification of anomalies, this approach enhances the efficiency and precision of the DQM process, ultimately improving the quality of the datasets used for analysis.

1 Introduction

The Compact Muon Solenoid (CMS) [4] is a general-purpose detector at the Large Hadron Collider (LHC) at CERN. CMS is designed to study high-energy proton-proton collisions, to better understand the fundamental forces and particles that make up the Universe. The CMS apparatus is composed of a complex system of sub-detectors to detect the particles produced in proton or ion collisions. The only particles that CMS cannot directly detect are neutrinos due to their very weak interaction with matter. To indirectly observe neutrinos, a kinematics observable called missing transverse energy (MET) is usually employed. MET is defined as:

$$\text{MET} = \Big| -\sum_i \boldsymbol{p}_{T,i} \Big|, \tag{1}$$

where $\boldsymbol{p}_{T,i}$ is the transverse momentum of the i-th reconstructed particle of the final state.

Since the transverse momentum of the initial state is null, according to the law of conservation of momentum and energy, MET is expected to vanish if all

W. Yin et al. (Eds.): IJCAI 2024, LNAI 14917, pp. 57–65, 2025.
https://doi.org/10.1007/978-981-97-9536-9_4

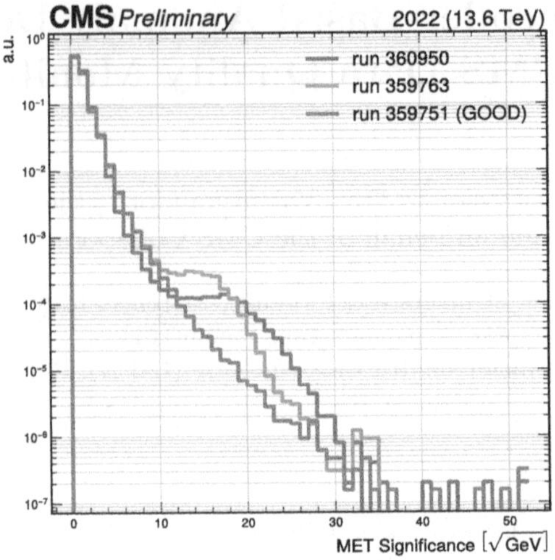

Fig. 1. Histograms of a Monitor Element (MET Significance) for three different runs, one flagged *GOOD* and two presenting an anomaly, therefore flagged *BAD*.

products of a collision are detected. However, because neutrinos and other weakly interacting particles can escape the detector without being directly detected, their presence results in a nonvanishing missing transverse energy value.

Particles with a color charge, such as quarks and gluons, cannot be directly observed. This is due to a fundamental principle known as color confinement, which states that color-charged particles cannot exist in isolation and must always combine in ways that result in an overall color-neutral charge. To comply with color confinement, quarks and gluons produced in strong interaction processes generate other colored particles, forming hadrons that cluster into *jets*, i.e., collimated groups of colorless objects [2].

The LHC's operation consists of several phases, which can be broken down into three main stages: the filling of the machine with proton beams (which takes minutes); the subsequent collision phase, in which the beams are brought into collision, which can last several hours, typically until the proton population in the beams has fallen below a predefined threshold; the beam dump, in which the remaining beams are dumped and the machine is cycled again. These three stages are collectively called in jargon a *fill*. CMS takes data during the collision phase of every fill and this data is gathered in "luminosity section", lumisections in short (LSs), that are sub-sections corresponding to around 23 s of data collection during which the instantaneous *luminosity* (a quantity related to the collision rate) is almost constant [4]. LSs are grouped in *runs*, of thousands of LSs.

Being CMS composed of various subsystems, each serving a specific purpose in particle detection and measurement, issues in the different sub-detectors can arise due to various factors, such as radiation damage, electronic noise, aging of components and temporary malfunctions (such as tripping of individual components). The monitoring of data quality is therefore crucial both online, during the data taking, to promptly spot issues and act on them, and offline, to provide analysts with datasets that are cleaned against the occasional failures that may have crept in. Data Certification (DC) is the final step of quality checks performed by Data Quality Monitoring (DQM) on recorded collision events. For each run, experts monitor several reconstructed distributions called Monitor Elements (MEs) to spot issues and anomalies in the data. For quantities pertaining to hadronic jets and MET, an issue in a few LSs could cause the entire run to be flagged as problematic (*BAD*) and thus removed from the pool of good-for-analysis data (*GOOD*).

Figure 1 shows the integrated (over the whole run) histogram illustrating a specific ME (MET Significance) for three distinct runs- one categorized as *GOOD* and the other two as *BAD*.

MET Significance is defined as:

$$\text{METSig} \equiv \frac{\text{MET}}{\sqrt{\text{SumET}}} = \frac{MET}{\sqrt{\sum_i |\boldsymbol{p}_{T,i}|}} \,. \tag{2}$$

This paper introduces a novel application of AutoEncoders (AEs) for anomaly detection within the CMS DQM framework. By exploiting unsupervised machine learning (ML) techniques, we aim to automate the identification of anomalous LSs. This approach enhances the efficiency and precision of the DQM process, allowing for the isolation and removal of problematic LSs, thereby improving the overall quality of datasets available for analysis. Our method demonstrates significant improvements in detecting subtle anomalies and ensures that data previously flagged as problematic can be refined and utilized effectively, ultimately contributing to more accurate and reliable physics analyses.

As the first automated technique at the per-LS level, our method offers clear time savings over manual analysis, with no prior ML methods for direct comparison. Future work will include evaluating our approach against other emerging ML techniques as they become available.

2 Methods

CMS has recently extended the capability of accumulating quantities monitored for data quality purposes per-LS to Jet and Missing Energy (JME) MEs. This capability allows for higher granularity in detecting anomalies, potentially enabling the saving of more data from runs presenting only a limited set of anomalous LSs. Given the high number (on the order of thousands) of LSs to be analyzed for each run, an automated approach for DC is required.

ML, particularly Neural Networks (NN) [8], can be implemented to this end. Therefore, to attack the problem, we employed unsupervised ML models based on AutoEncoders (AE) [9].

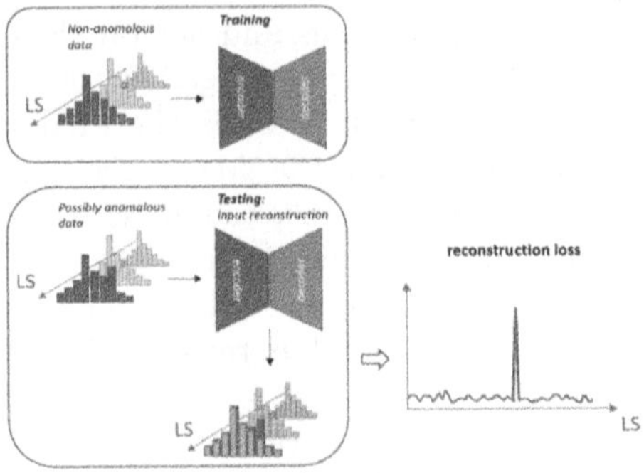

Fig. 2. Scheme of training and testing steps for the models

2.1 Input Data and Preprocessing

Given a specific ME, the input features to our models consist of bins of the corresponding histogram, with each LS being a single time sample. The binning is defined a priori based on the specific MEs and is determined by the experimental setup. Thus, data is structured in the shape ($\#bins, \#LS$). Before feeding the models with training (and testing) data we performed rescaling in the $[0, 1]$ interval. This is a common practice for these kinds of models. Different rescalings are possible, but one that we found very effective is the following bin-by-bin rescaling:

$$\hat{x}_{\text{train}} = \frac{x_{\text{train}} - \min(x_{\text{train}})}{\max(x_{\text{train}}) - \min(x_{\text{train}})}, \tag{3}$$

where the maximum and minimum are computed along the time direction.

2.2 Models

Two types of AutoEncoders (AEs) were developed: a dense Under-complete AE and a Long Short-Term Memory (LSTM) Under-complete AE. An Under-complete AE refers to an architecture where the number of nodes decreases in the encoder layers and then increases in the decoder layers.

The first model that was optimized is a dense Under-complete AE [9] built using dense layers with three hidden layers in total, see Fig. 3. The number of nodes inside the layer after the input layer (`encoding_dim_1`) and the number of nodes inside the central layer (`encoding_dim_2`) are two hyper-parameters of the model.

The second model is the more complex LSTM Under-complete AE [10] schematized in Fig. 4. This model is designed to handle sequential data, making it suitable for the time-series nature of DQM metrics. The use of LSTM nodes allows the model to capture temporal dependencies within the data, providing a more accurate representation for time-series analysis.

The structure is analogous to the dense Under-complete AE, with two hyper-parameters for the number of nodes in the hidden layers. However, each node

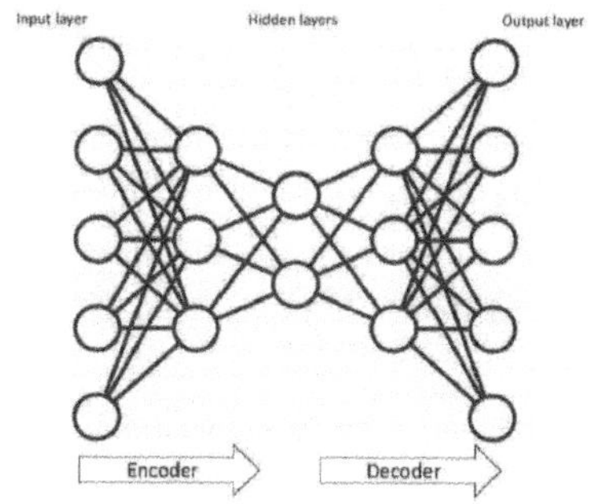

Fig. 3. Structure of the dense Under-complete AE (the number of nodes is just indicative, `encoding_dim_1` = 3, `encoding_dim_2` = 2)

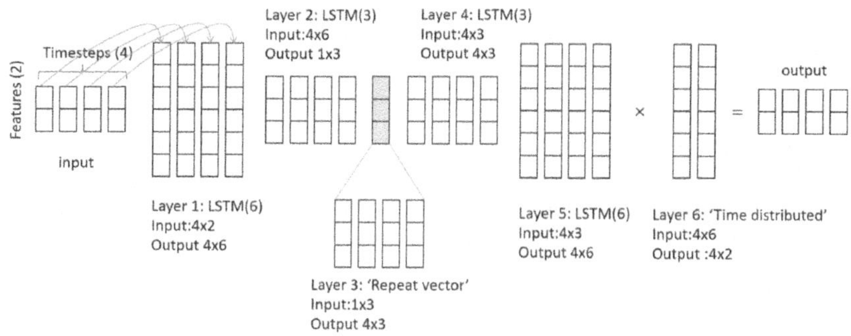

Fig. 4. Structure of the LSTM Under-complete AE (the number of nodes and the size of the window are just indicative, `encoding_dim_1` = 6, `encoding_dim_2` = 3 and `window_size` = 4)

in this model is an LSTM node, which stands for Long Short-Term Memory recurrent neural network (RNN). Due to the recurrent nature of LSTM, each node processes not a single time sample but a sequence of samples defined by the hyperparameter `window_size`. Consequently, the output of each layer is duplicated and fed into every node of the following layer. For the latent layer, a `RepeatVector` layer is used to replicate the latent vector, enabling the subsequent decoding layers to process these copies.

The choice of these two models was driven by their complementary strengths. The dense Under-complete AE is simpler and faster to train, making it suitable for initial anomaly detection tasks. On the other hand, the LSTM Under-complete AE is more adept at capturing temporal patterns within the data, which is critical given the time-series nature of the input features.

2.3 Training and Testing

Both the models were trained on non-anomalous data from *GOOD* runs: histograms of specific MEs are fed to the model with per-LS granularity to allow the AE to learn a normal, non-anomalous behavior of that specific ME, see Fig. 2. The training is performed via the minimization of the reconstruction loss, a measure of the distance between the input and output of the AE. In this case, the reconstruction loss is the mean squared error (MSE):

$$\mathrm{MSE} = \frac{1}{n}\sum_{i=1}^{n}\left(y_i - \hat{y}_i\right)^2, \tag{4}$$

where y and $\hat{y}$ are respectively the input and the output of the AE, and n is the bin number.

Possibly anomalous runs under investigation are tested by examining again the reconstruction loss: peaks and steps in this function indicate LSs containing histograms that deviate from the learned behavior.

2.4 Optimization

Each model is optimized individually for each ME by training on a reference *GOOD* run and validating it on a collection $\mathcal{C}$ of N known anomalous runs. The chosen metric, $\eta = \sum_i \eta_i$, $i \in [1, N]$, increases with the size of the step/peak in the reconstruction loss when the anomaly occurs and decreases with the standard deviation of the reconstruction loss in non-anomalous regions:

$$\eta_i = \frac{\mid mean\left(\mathrm{MSE_{anom}}\right) - mean\left(\mathrm{MSE_{no\text{-}anom}}\right) \mid}{stddev\left(\mathrm{MSE_{no\text{-}anom}}\right)}. \tag{5}$$

The hyper-parameters optimized for the dense model were `encoding_dim_1`, `encoding_dim_2` and `batch_size`, while for the LSTM model, the `window_size` of the LSTM layers was also used. The optimization was performed using the automatic hyperparameter optimization software framework *Optuna*, exploiting the TPE (Tree-structured Parzen Estimator) sampler and the Hyperband Pruner technologies [1]. Based on the reconstruction loss of the optimized models on $\mathcal{C}$, a threshold value, denoted as `thr`, was associated with each model. During testing, if the reconstruction loss surpasses this threshold, it is flagged as anomalous, prompting the removal of the corresponding LSs.

3 Results

The models are tested in this example on a run (360950) that was flagged *BAD* by JME due to the presence of an anomaly visible in histograms of many different MEs, see e.g., Fig. 1. The training is performed on a reference run (*GOOD*) characterized by operational conditions analogous to those of the run being tested. By analyzing the per-LS MET Significance for the run via the dense Undercomplete AE, a peak is observed in the reconstruction loss corresponding to a specific LS (Fig. 5a). The threshold for this model, $\mathtt{thr}_{\mathrm{dense}} = 0.1$, is passed. Once the anomalous LS is identified, it is removed from the run. The resulting histogram for the *BAD* run shows how the cause of the MET Significance anomaly was isolated to a specific LS, as shown in Fig. 5b: the exclusion of the identified anomalous LS results in the remaining data no longer exhibiting the anomaly.

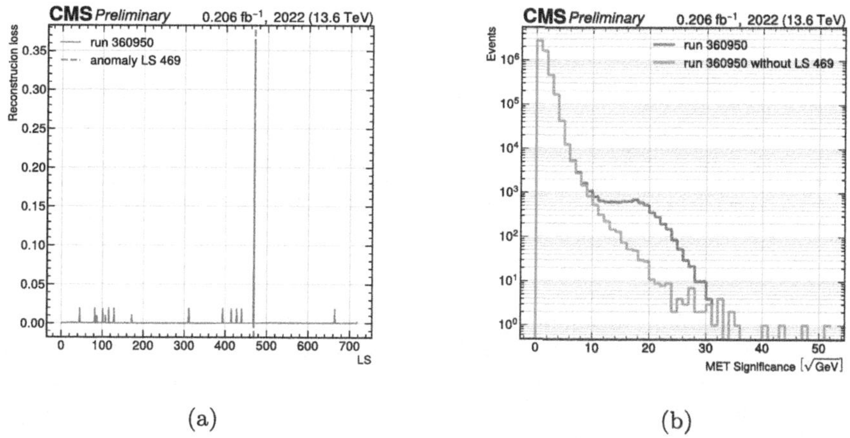

Fig. 5. (a) Reconstruction loss by the dense Under-complete model for an anomalous run showing a high peak corresponding to LS 469. and (b) histogram of the same run before and after the removal of the identified anomalous LS

As a second example, we consider a run presenting (in its integrated histogram) an analogous anomaly, Fig. 6a. When tested with the dense Under-complete model, only a major peak in the reconstruction loss is visible, along with smaller peaks that are not relevant according to the predefined threshold, as shown in Fig. 6b. We emphasise that for single LS anomalies, comparing the anomalous run with the average along the time direction of a *GOOD* training run using MSE is generally sufficient to identify the issue: this is evident in Fig. 6b for the first peak. When the only relevant LS is removed, the resulting histogram still presents an anomalous shape, as shown in Fig. 6a. Since manually decreasing the threshold allows for the removal of the entire anomaly (as a second peak is considered), we decided to test the more complex LSTM Under-complete AE on the run. The resulting reconstruction loss shows a more pronounced peak for a second LS, which is acceptable according to the threshold for the model, $\mathtt{thr}_{\mathrm{LSTM}} = 0.1$, as shown in Fig. 6b. The removal of both major peaks results in the complete elimination of the anomaly, as shown in Fig. 6a. It is important to stress that for this second anomaly, comparing the run with the average of the training run is not sufficient to highlight it.

Upon inspecting the two identified LSs, it is apparent that both anomalies were affecting the same set of bins in the histograms, with the second one being less pronounced: this results in a suppression of the magnitude of the rescaled bins after (3), making the anomaly less visible to both models.

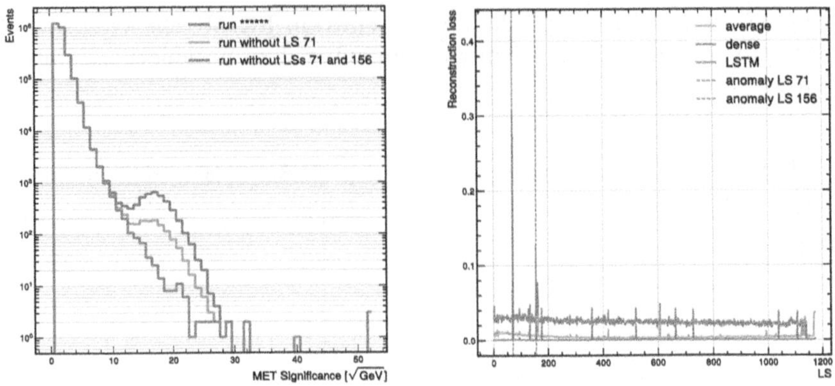

(a) (b)

Fig. 6. (a) Histogram of an anomalous run before and after the removal of the identified anomalous LSs. The orange histogram represents the result after removing the LS identified by the dense Under-complete model, while the green one shows the result after removing both LSs identified by the LSTM Under-complete model. (b) Reconstruction loss comparison between the dense Under-complete model (blue), the MSE comparison with the average of the training run (orange), and the LSTM Under-complete model (green) for an anomalous run. Both the dense model and the comparison with the average exhibit a prominent peak at LS 71, surpassing our predefined anomaly threshold. Meanwhile, the LSTM model displays both a significant peak at LS 71 and a secondary, albeit less pronounced, peak at LS 156, both exceeding our anomaly threshold for the model. (Color figure online)

4 Conclusions

An AutoEncoder-based anomaly detection tool has been successfully developed and tested for Data Quality Monitoring (DQM) in the CMS experiment. This tool, capable of detecting anomalies at the granularity of individual luminosity sections (LSs), significantly improves the data certification process by isolating problematic LSs within runs that were flagged as *BAD*.

While some anomalies could be detected through straightforward statistical comparisons, such as evaluating deviations from average values, these methods often miss more subtle anomalies that can significantly impact data quality. The models presented in this paper, particularly the LSTM Under-complete AutoEncoder, demonstrate a greater capability to identify such subtle anomalies by learning complex patterns within the data. This enhances overall data quality by allowing more accurate identification and removal of problematic LSs. The removal of identified anomalous LSs ensures that the remaining data is reliable, thus recovering data that would otherwise be discarded. This approach not only streamlines the DQM process but also increases the efficiency and accuracy of data used for physics analyses.

To thoroughly understand the contributions of individual components and model variations, an ablation study can be conducted in future work. This study would involve systematically removing or altering components of the models to evaluate their impact on performance, thereby providing deeper insights into the effectiveness of each model component.

Even though machine learning and deep learning have been employed in high-energy physics (HEP) for physics analysis [6], and in particular for anomaly detection [3, 7], this work represents one of the first instances of their application in DQM. The successful implementation of machine learning techniques, as demonstrated here, highlights their potential in enhancing the robustness and reliability of data quality monitoring in HEP experiments.

This work utilizes results that are part of a CMS Detector Performance Note (DP-note) [5].

Disclosure of Interests. The authors have no competing interests to declare that are relevant to the content of this article.

References

1. Akiba, T., Sano, S., Yanase, T., Ohta, T., Koyama, M.: Optuna: a next-generation hyperparameter optimization framework. In: Proceedings of the 25th ACM SIGKDD International Conference on Knowledge Discovery & Data Mining, pp. 2623–2631 (2019)
2. Ali, A., Kramer, G.: Jets and QCD: a historical review of the discovery of the quark and gluon jets and its impact on QCD. Eur. Phys. J. H **36**, 245–326 (2011)
3. Belis, V., Odagiu, P., Aarrestad, T.K.: Machine learning for anomaly detection in particle physics. Rev. Phys. **12**, 100091 (2024)
4. CMS Collaboration: S08004. JINST **3** (2008)
5. CMS Collaboration: An autoencoder-based anomaly detection tool with a per-LS granularity. Technical report 2023/010, CMS DP (2023)
6. D'Agnolo, R.T., Wulzer, A.: Learning new physics from a machine. Phys. Rev. D **99**, 015014 (2019). https://doi.org/10.1103/PhysRevD.99.015014
7. Gandrakota, A., et al.: Robust anomaly detection for particle physics using multi-background representation learning. arXiv preprint arXiv:2401.08777 (2024)
8. Goodfellow, I., et al.: Deep Learning. MIT Press, Cambridge (2016)
9. Hinton, G.E., Salakhutdinov, R.R.: Reducing the dimensionality of data with neural networks. Science **313**(5786), 504–507 (2006)
10. Wei, Y., Jang-Jaccard, J., Xu, W., Sabrina, F., Camtepe, S., Boulic, M.: LSTM-autoencoder-based anomaly detection for indoor air quality time-series data. IEEE Sens. J. **23**(4), 3787–3800 (2023)

Democracy and AI

Using LLMs to Structure and Visualize Policy Discourse

Aaditya Bhatia[1,2] and Gita Sukthankar[2](✉)

[1] United States Military Academy, West Point, NY 10996, USA
aaditya.bhatia@westpoint.edu
[2] University of Central Florida, Orlando, FL 32816, USA
{aadityabhatia,gita.sukthankar}@ucf.edu

Abstract. Public deliberation forums produce copious amounts of unorganized textual data reflecting diverse viewpoints. Visualization can serve as a valuable tool for understanding the relationships between policy preferences. We introduce a unique approach to visualizing opinion data gathered from the Polis online platform in which LLMs are used to generate positions and structure the data into argument maps. Each AI-generated position is supported by human-generated statements, providing a more meaningful organization of Polis's opinion data. We believe that these argument maps can provide policymakers with easy-to-understand visualizations that summarize public sentiment.

Keywords: LLMs · argument mapping · computational democracy

1 Introduction

Deliberative democracy encourages participants to reflect on various perspectives and form an informed opinion through evidence and reasoning. It assumes that through rational discourse, participants can arrive at decisions that are more legitimate and informed [11]. Such discourse can be effectively organized into an argument map, which visually represents the flow of information [5], as explored by Klein [6], emphasizing the significance of crowd-scale deliberation in tackling complex issues. Platforms like Polis [9] provide a scalable way to gauge public opinion using real-time voting and commenting. Our experimental approach leverages Large Language Models (LLMs) to organize this unstructured opinion data into visually appealing argument maps.

Starting with a set of publicly available Polis datasets, we review discussion events held by various organizations. Using various transformer models, we calculate embeddings for all statements, cluster similar data points and identify latent topics within the dataset through topic modeling. We then identify problems and proposed solutions, and use those to craft actionable positions or *insights* aimed at driving policy changes. Then we visualize these insights using *argument maps*—a set of discussion trees that organize these statements hierarchically, demonstrating the collection of human-generated statements that

W. Yin et al. (Eds.): IJCAI 2024, LNAI 14917, pp. 69–76, 2025.
https://doi.org/10.1007/978-981-97-9536-9_5

support each of the AI-generated insights, providing a meaningful categorization of statements. Finally, we use a scoring technique to surface the most valuable insights. Our methodology is designed to uncover and identify insights with the highest levels of public acceptance, thereby facilitating a comprehensive understanding of the public opinion data and aiding in well-informed conclusions.

2 Related Work

The integration of LLMs in the realm of policy decision-making, particularly in conjunction with the principles of collective intelligence, carries significant potential yet remains underexplored. While there is a robust body of literature on the usage of LLMs for a variety of practical applications [8] and on the fundamentals of collective intelligence [7], the effective amalgamation of these two domains in policymaking contexts is not extensively studied. The work of Small et al. [10] touches upon the capabilities of LLMs to process, structure, and interpret large-scale public opinion data for informing policy decisions. This paper builds upon their work by providing a detailed pipeline on the usage of LLMs for generating argument maps. Software agents carry the potential to drastically enrich the deliberative process through argument mapping [1]. These agents not only facilitate the capture and organization of complex discussions but also ensure that related discourse across topics is interlinked and easily navigable, thereby enhancing the depth and breadth of analysis. Moreover, the role of automated facilitation agents in enhancing the deliberative process is notably illustrated in several works [3,4].

3 Method

Datasets. Our research focuses on two sets of events from the Polis dataset: *american-assembly.bowling-green* and *scoop-hivemind*. The first one originates from a conversation facilitated by the American Assembly in Bowling Green, Kentucky in 2018. This dataset explores local and regional perspectives regarding the city's well-being and probes the narrative of a divided America. It comprises 896 comments, of which 289 were moderated out, leaving a substantial 607 comments for analysis. This dataset is particularly valuable for understanding community priorities and perceptions at a local level. The second set, *scoop-hivemind*, stems from multiple conversations conducted by New Zealand's Public Engagement Projects (PEP) in partnership with the news outlet Scoop regarding issues of national significance. It consists of a total of 752 comments submitted by 96 people, with 294 comments moderated out, resulting in 458 accepted comments. These datasets include detailed voting data accounting for each *agree* or *disagree* vote cast by the participants.

Language Model Interaction. To manage text generation from our language models, we use the *guidance* framework originally developed by Microsoft. It represents a unique programming paradigm that enhances control and efficiency by constraining generation through regular expressions and context-free grammar. Figure 1 shows how developers can freely add text at any point between text generations, effectively interleaving control and generation seamlessly using traditional programming paradigms such as conditionals and loops.

Insight Generation. An insight is a position that advocates for specific actions to address identified issues or implement solutions. This paper proposes a unique approach, outlined in Fig. 2, to synthesize insights by interpreting the statements posted by humans without introducing new ideas or concepts. First, using the BERTopic framework [2], we cluster the statements into separate topics and identify representative phrases for each of them. To ensure fair representation, we calculate an *agreeability* factor for each statement, defined as the ratio of *agree* votes to the total votes. For each topic, we prompt the LLM with each topic's representative keywords and statements with *agreeability* above a set threshold, and ask it to identify potential areas for improvements. In a second set of instructions, as shown in Fig. 1, we prompt the model with each listed area of improvement and ask it to identify the most significant problem and proposed solution from within the user statements.

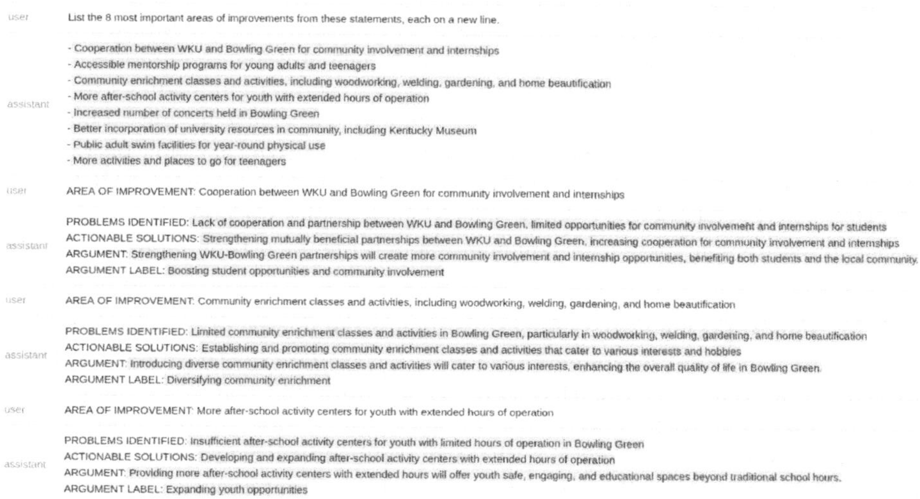

Fig. 1. The set of instructions and prompts used to generate insights using *Guidance* framework. Text highlighted in green was produced by LLM, while everything else was programmatically inserted into the LLM context. Guidance enables developers to intertwine text and generation, allowing precise control of language model contexts. (Color figure online)

We do this to ensure that the model does not generate its own content, but rather helps interpret the information already present in the public opinion dataset. Finally, we feed this information back to the language model to synthesize positions. This results in an actionable set of positions that advocate for a change or improvement.

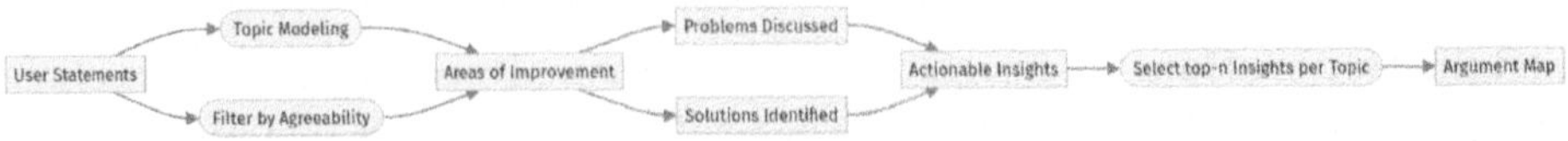

Fig. 2. Insight generation pipeline demonstrates how user-generated comments are used to synthesize actionable positions, which in turn are scored and sorted to generate argument maps.

Insight-Statement Association. After generating coherent insights, we aim to quantify the support behind each of these positions. We have the voting data for individual statements but not the generated positions. Correlating voting data requires a precise characterization of the semantic relationship between original statements and the newly formed insights. To accomplish this, we experiment with several techniques with varying degrees of success. First, given a set of insights from a topic, we use the language model to sequentially consider individual statements from that topic and select an insight that the statement most closely supports. This paradigm assumes that each statement supports exactly one position, which is often not true. Second, we use text embeddings to determine which statements are most closely aligned with each insight. Third, we frame this as a three-class classification task to categorize each link between an LLM-generated insight and a human-generated statement as either SUPPORT, REFUTE, or UNRELATED. From within each topic, we present every possible insight-statement pair to a language model, one at a time, and ask for the classification.

Insight Scoring. Our next task is to estimate the degree of consensus behind each of our generated arguments. We use the available voting data to determine which statements support or refute a position and count the unique participants endorsing these statements. Counting the number of participants who agree versus those who disagree with each argument mitigates the influence of highly active individuals that tend to vote on lots of statements, and thus more accurately estimates the consensus as opposed to the raw number of votes. We estimate an *acceptance* factor as an approximation of the ratio of people who would potentially agree with the argument given their vote on the statement.

Argument Mapping. The final part of the pipeline involves visually depicting the relationship between different entities on an argument map to articulate and display the structure and interconnections of insights and statements within a given context. Argdown is a simple Markdown-inspired syntax for analyzing complex argumentation structures. We developed a reduced grammatical specification API for Argdown in Python, which abstracts the syntax and produces a simple but valid argument map. To produce the maps, we iterate over our list of topics and select the top three insights from each. Then we select the three most highly voted comments that support each argument. Each position is connected to its parent topic, while each statement is connected to the position that it supports. This creates a three-layer hierarchy, where the topics are shown in the topmost layer, AI-generated insights are placed in the middle, and human-generated supporting statements are at the bottom. The links in the map are strictly for SUPPORT relationships since we treat REFUTE relationships as noise pending further evaluation.

4 Results

Insight-Statement Association. Associating insights with individual statements is a crucial part of our pipeline since it enables us to measure the support behind each insight and prioritize the ones with the highest levels of consensus. We experimented with three techniques to deduce this association. The simplest option is to present all insights from a given topic to the LLM at once and ask it to associate each statement to the most semantically related insight. This technique, despite being simple, produced very unreliable results. This was likely caused by excessive amounts of text in the model's context window, which severely impacted its reasoning abilities. The second technique involved using text embeddings to find the most closely aligned statements. This reliably produced a list of semantically related insight-statement pairs, but it did not indicate whether the two had a SUPPORT or REFUTE relationship, or even if one logically followed the other. While embeddings reliably identify semantic similarity, they fail to provide any additional context into the association. The third technique, as shown in Fig. 3, framed the problem as a three-class classification task

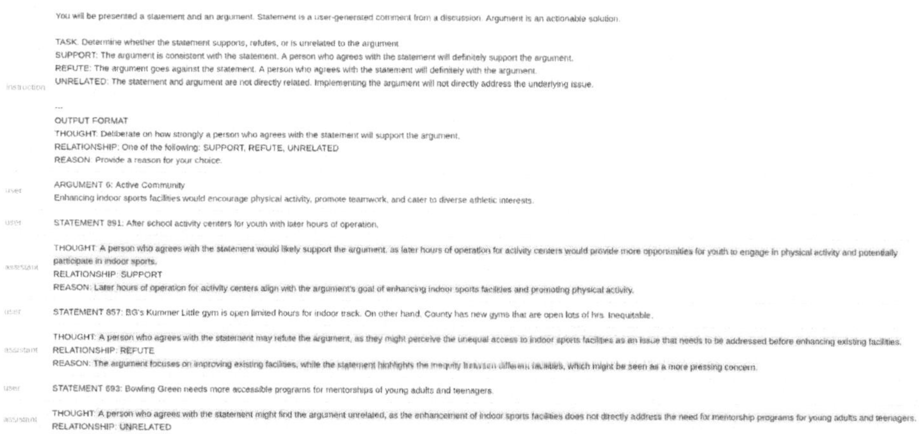

Fig. 3. LLM instructions to characterize relationship between insights and statements using chain-of-thought reasoning. Text highlighted in green was generated by LLM, while everything else was programmatically inserted into the LLM context. (Color figure online)

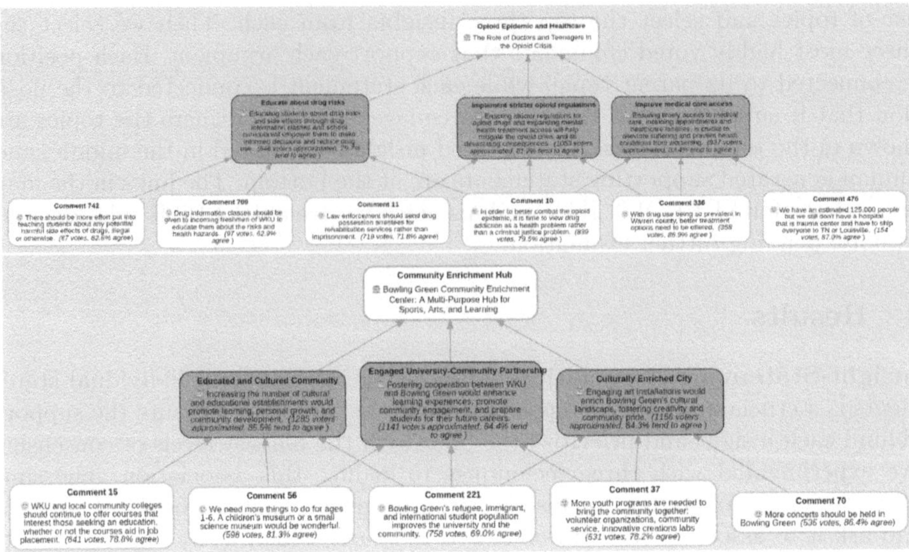

Fig. 4. Argument maps generated using *american-assembly.bowling-green* dataset covering two different topics. The upper map addresses healthcare and the opioid epidemic, while the lower focuses on community enrichment programs. The middle row in each map contains LLM-generated insights, while the lowest row has human-authored statements that support one or more of the insights. We use Polis voting data to estimate the potential agreement for each generated insight. (Color figure online)

and yielded the best results. The instruction prompt specified that the model should only indicate SUPPORT if a person who agrees with the statement will definitely support the insight. We also used a chain-of-thought reasoning technique, allowing the model to articulate its reasoning before rendering a decision. Applying this process to every possible insight-statement combination is very computationally expensive but yielded the most reliable results. We recommend a combination of second and third techniques to develop a more efficient pipeline with improved accuracy.

Argument Mapping. Figure 4 shows two argument maps generated using our pipeline. The first one addresses healthcare issues in the city of Bowling Green, while the second focuses on community enrichment programs. In each of the trees, the top row shows the BERTopic-discovered topics, while the AI-generated arguments are placed in the middle row; both feature a robot icon to clearly indicate their non-human origin. Human-generated supporting statements are placed in the bottom row along with a smiley that denotes human authorship.

5 Conclusion

This paper tackles the challenge of structuring online discourse to distill large amounts of opinion data into coherent, actionable insights, promising to significantly enhance policymakers' ability to understand and respond to public opinion and lead to more informed and democratic decision-making processes. We demonstrated a scalable and flexible software pipeline for retrospective data analysis of deliberation events.[1] Although generating text using LLMs carries the risk of hallucinations, our incremental approach provides guard rails to prevent the language models from inventing new data.

Our work faced several limitations around the sensitivity of various models to prompt changes and inability to handle complex instructions, requiring smaller and simpler prompts to ensure accuracy. Future work will focus on extracting issues, claims, and positions from individual statements and connecting ideas across disparate statements and topics, enabling deeper insights into public discussions. This alignment between public sentiment and policy action would not only enhance the legitimacy of democratic institutions but also ensure that governance is more responsive, informed, and inclusive. Ultimately, we hope that this research will result in tools that better assist policymakers and leaders in making efficient and equitable decisions that improve consensus and engagement.

Acknowledgments. This material is based upon work partially supported by the Defense Advanced Research Projects Agency (DARPA) under Contract No. W911NF-20-1-0008. The conclusions and opinions expressed in this research paper are those of the authors and do not necessarily reflect the official policy or position of the U.S. Government or Department of Defense.

Disclosure of Interests. The authors have no competing interests to declare that are relevant to the content of this article.

References

1. Buckingham Shum, S., Sierhuis, M., Park, J., Brown, M.: Software agents in support of human argument mapping. In: Proceedings of the Conference on Computational Models of Argument: Proceedings of COMMA 2010, pp. 123–134. IOS Press, NLD, August 2010. https://doi.org/10.3233/978-1-60750-618-8-123
2. Grootendorst, M.: BERTopic: neural topic modeling with a class-based TF-IDF procedure, March 2022. http://arxiv.org/abs/2203.05794, arXiv:2203.05794 [cs]
3. Hadfi, R., Ito, T.: Augmented democratic deliberation: can conversational agents boost deliberation in social media? In: Proceedings of the 21st International Conference on Autonomous Agents and Multiagent Systems, AAMAS 2022, pp. 1794–1798. International Foundation for Autonomous Agents and Multiagent Systems, Richland, SC, May 2022
4. Ito, T., Hadfi, R., Suzuki, S.: An agent that facilitates crowd discussion. Group Decis. Negot. **31**(3), 621–647 (2022)

[1] The source code is publicly available at: github.com/aadityabhatia/polis-argmap/.

5. Kirschner, P.A., Buckingham Shum, S.J., Carr, C.S., Diaper, D., Sanger, C. (eds.): Visualizing Argumentation: Software Tools for Collaborative and Educational Sense-Making. Computer Supported Cooperative Work. Springer, London (2003). https://doi.org/10.1007/978-1-4471-0037-9. http://link.springer.com/10.1007/978-1-4471-0037-9
6. Klein, M.: Crowd-Scale Deliberation For Complex Problems: A Progress Report (2022)
7. Malone, T.W.: How can human-computer "Superminds" develop business strategies? In: Canals, J., Heukamp, F. (eds.) The Future of Management in an AI World. IBC, pp. 165–183. Springer, Cham (2020). https://doi.org/10.1007/978-3-030-20680-2_9. http://link.springer.com/10.1007/978-3-030-20680-2_9
8. Pan, J.Z., et al.: Large language models and knowledge graphs: opportunities and challenges, August 2023. https://doi.org/10.48550/arXiv.2308.06374, http://arxiv.org/abs/2308.06374, arXiv:2308.06374 [cs]
9. Small, C.: Polis: scaling deliberation by mapping high dimensional opinion spaces. RECERCA. Revista de Pensament i Anàlisi (2021)
10. Small, C.T., et al.: Opportunities and risks of LLMs for scalable deliberation with Polis, June 2023. http://arxiv.org/abs/2306.11932, arXiv:2306.11932 [cs]
11. Williams, A.E.: Are wicked problems a lack of general collective intelligence? AI Society **38**(1), 343–348 (2023)

Participatory Budgeting as an Element of Crowdsourcing in the Smart City Area

Łukasz Przysucha(✉)

Wroclaw University of Economics and Business, Komandorska 118/120, 53-345 Wroclaw, Poland
lukasz.przysucha@ue.wroc.pl

Abstract. The work discusses the area of crowdsourcing in a smart city on the example of participatory budgeting. Using the PLS-SEM model, factors that influence the willingness of residents to share knowledge with decision-makers were identified.

Keywords: Crowdsourcing · Smart City · PLS-SEM · participatory budgeting

1 Introduction

Since the beginning of the second half of the 20th century, there has been a rapid development of technology, globalization is progressing significantly and the development of urban areas is visible. According to United Nations data [1], in 2018, 4.2 billion people in the world (55% of the population) lived in urban areas. It is forecast that in 2050, urban areas will be inhabited by 6.7 billion people (68% of the population), which shows how important an aspect of our civilization is urbanization and its final form, cities. Nowadays, the term "smart city" is used more and more often on various levels. It is a term [2] defining a certain idea and style of functioning of the city and the community inhabiting it (smart societies). Currently, smart cities include not only technologies such as Big Data, 5G Internet, IoT or AI solutions, but also communication between decision-makers and residents, which in the form of proactive interaction supports the perception of problems in cities and effectively solves them. One of the tools for efficient communication between residents and decision-makers.

and other stakeholders operating in the city area may be crowdsourcing. It is the process of assigning tasks to a wide group of people and proposing solutions to achieve the organizer's specific goals [3]. The most popular representative of crowdsourcing in cities is participatory budgeting, which allows communication between decision-makers, urban stakeholders and residents. It obtains information about the needs of residents [4]. In this work, the author focused on the analysis of factors that influence residents to be more willing to share their knowledge with decision-makers.

W. Yin et al. (Eds.): IJCAI 2024, LNAI 14917, pp. 77–85, 2025.
https://doi.org/10.1007/978-981-97-9536-9_6

2 Smart City

The term smart city refers not only to urban architecture or infrastructure. It is interdisciplinary [5]. There is no one specific definition that fully defines the idea, concepts and schemes of a smart city. Over the years, various terms and philosophies have been created to describe agglomerations and urban structures that interact with society and technologies. R. Giffinger defines [6] Smart City as a well-functioning city built on an “intelligent” combination of qualifications and actions of self-deciding, independent and aware citizens. In turn, P. Lombardi et al. indicates [7] that a smart city is one that has an educated society, is developing and focuses on communication channels between local administration and residents. When reviewing the definitions and analyzes of smart cities, it can be assumed that smart cities are defined primarily by conscious citizens living in them. Four generations of smart cities have been defined in the literature. Smart City 1.0 is the earliest form of creating smart cities. The role of the initiator and leader of the project falls to a corporation or business entity, usually from the ICT area due to its activity in the area of new technologies. This generation is called *technology driven* [8]. Smart city 2.0 – this is the second generation of smart cities, which is assumed to be controlled by city authorities. All projects are initiated by offices and local authorities, responsible for creating the vision of given projects, organizing financial resources for their implementation and consulting with experts specializing in the specific areas of the implemented initiatives. Smart city 3.0 - this is another perspective of creating smart cities, which is characterized by focusing on the creativity and needs of residents [9]. The city’s role is no longer to decide on infrastructure and social plans, but only to co-decide and support the decision-making process of residents. Recently, another approach to city development has appeared, called smart city 4.0 [10]. It is a concept in which the city is a sustainable [11], constantly developing ecosystem in which ICT solutions support communication between decision-makers and residents and stakeholders and optimize the operation of urban infrastructure [12]. This means that currently smart cities focus mainly on the community, its development and problems. Technologies and ICT solutions support this process and are an integral element of the implementation of new solutions for people. Smart cities can be given dimensions or their components can be distinguished [13]. S. Dirks and M. Keeling point [14] to the importance of organic integration of various urban systems (business, transport, city services, residents, energy, water, communication), emphasizing that one of the connectors between areas is information and communication technology. The author analyzed the most common areas of a smart city in the literature. These are: economy, management, environment, mobility, people and quality of life. All these areas have in common the fact that smart city projects are planned and implemented in their areas. Smart city projects are initiatives aimed at using advanced information and communication technologies to improve efficiency, sustainable development and the quality of life of residents in cities [15,16]. These projects introduce innovative solutions such as the Internet of Things (IoT), data analysis, artificial intelligence, and monitoring systems to create an intelligent, integrated and dynamic urban environment. Projects supporting communication between decision-makers, stakeholders and residents are extremely important. Due to their importance, more and more smart cities are deciding to implement them. These projects are in the area of crowdsourcing, which is described in detail in the second section.

3 Crowdsourcing and Participatory Budgeting

Crowdsourcing is a relatively new field of research. Due to its increasingly frequent use in various areas of human activity, researchers consider it a very interesting scientific object. The term crowdsourcing itself was first used by the editors of Wired magazine - J. Howe and M. Robinson [17]. It described the process of companies outsourcing work to crowds. In the same year, J. Howe published the definition of crowdsourcing on his blog [18]: "In simple terms, crowdsourcing is an activity in which a company or institution takes over a function that was once performed by employees and outsources it to an undefined (and generally large) network of people in the form of an open recruitment. This can take the form of peer production (when work is done collectively), but is also often undertaken by individuals. An essential prerequisite is the use of an open call format and a large network of potential employees".

Based on the collected definitions, it can be concluded that crowdsourcing is the process of entrusting the performance of a given task or a series of tasks by a client to a given individual or crowd (group of individuals) [19, 20]. It is usually announced and carried out remotely, online, using the latest technologies. The original concept of crowdsourcing mainly referred to the delegation of work in the area of enterprises [21], but now crowdsourcing has wider applications - it can be used in organizations, universities, cities and other areas gathering people [22].

The author notes [19] that the willingness to use crowdsourcing may result from a lack of knowledge. In the case of a smart city, the analysis covers, among others: flow of knowledge between decision-makers (local administration) and residents. The lack of knowledge about the needs of residents in the area of local administration necessitates the need for decision-makers to acquire knowledge, e.g., using crowdsourcing [23]. The mentioned crowdsourcing uses the latest ICT technologies and tools such as the Internet, social media and mobile applications. Electronic tools are an essential element supporting the development of this initiative. Crowdsourcing unlocks residents' involvement, which is closely related to residents' motivation. The involvement of citizens and the willingness to exchange and share information develop citizens' knowledge [24], which - together with experienced administration - builds collective intelligence, which is a form of crowdsourcing. This means that crowdsourcing operates on tools that support exchange between residents, stakeholders and residents. The factors indicated in the model, properly implemented in the smart city environment, can increase residents' involvement in social participation and use of the residents' budget. This was also verified on the basis of in-depth interviews with decision-makers from Wroclaw (Poland) and Montpellier (France) in the author's doctoral thesis.

An example of a smart city project that fits into the assumptions of crowdsourcing is participatory budgeting, which enables dialogue with residents, provides decision-makers with information about the needs of residents and effectively changes both urban infrastructure and society thanks to the submitted and implemented projects in his area [25].

Research on participatory budgeting is part of a broader area of interest in democratic innovations, both theoretical and practical. The current shape of the entire tool supporting participatory budgeting and the process itself fit into the idea of a smart city as a crowdsourcing project.

Participatory budgeting is a democratic process that allows residents to participate in the discussion and have direct influence on decisions regarding the public budget [26, 27]. Throughout the budget construction process, residents consider spending priorities and vote on how the budget should be divided among various public projects. These funds are allocated to the implementation of social initiatives submitted by citizens [4].

4 PLS-SEM Model

The author focused on the analysis of factors influencing the willingness of residents to share knowledge with decision-makers using the example of the use of a participatory budget. In this work, the author presents the results obtained during a study conducted in Wroclaw (Poland) in 2021 on a sample of 317 residents. This model was taken from the author's doctoral thesis. To confirm, a study was conducted in Montpellier (France) on a sample of 306 residents, where the results showed similar observations and conclusions. The sample size was selected based on indications in the literature in the area of PLS-SEM. The study applied the 10-times rule, used, among others, by M. Mahadzirah et al. [28], J. Hair et al. [29], which suggests that the minimum sample size should be equal to 10 times the number of independent variables in the most complex regression in the PLS path model (taking into account structural and measurement models).

Partial least squares structural equation modeling (PLS-SEM) is one of the most frequently used methods of analyzing multidimensional data among scientists dealing with business and social sciences. This modeling is based on the method of estimating composite (formative) or latent (reflective) variables. Data analysis and preparation of some reports were performed in the SmartPLS application version 4.0.8.4.

The proposed model, based on the example of the cities of Wroclaw and Montpellier, consists of 11 constructs: self-efficacy (SE), effort expectancy (EE), perceived security (PS), perceived privacy (PP), trust in government (TG), trust in technology (TT), price value (PV), self-concern (SC), other-orientation (OO), group oriented (GO) and behavioral intention (BI). They were taken from the UTAUT2 model, from literature [30–32], own research and in-depth individual interviews.

Manifest variables identified and used in other research works in the scientific literature were assigned to the operationalization of each latent variable.

The main construct indicating the result of the analysis is *behavioral intention*, which indicates the individual's readiness to implement a specific behavior. Behavioral intention is believed to immediately precede the behavior [33]. Another construct - *self-efficacy* can be the basis for motivation, well-being and personal achievements. It is a person's particular set of beliefs that determines how well a plan of action can be carried out in future situations. A person with high self-efficacy sees challenges as things to be mastered rather than threats to be avoided [34]. *Perceived security* is the degree to which users (residents) believe that crowdsourcing services are safe in terms of storing and sharing confidential data [35]. In the aspect of research on crowdsourcing in the area of a smart city, this factor refers to an online platform supporting information exchange processes between residents and decision-makers. *Perceived privacy* is the degree to which users believe that a given technology or solution is smart and will protect their personal data. Existing research has shown that privacy is one of the biggest concerns of users using smart services [36]. Perceived privacy threats can significantly impact trust [37]. *Trust in government* is defined as the social assessment of decision-makers based on the perception of the degree of honesty of political authorities, agencies and institutions, as well as the ability to provide services in line with citizens' expectations. In turn, in terms of the next construct, S. Peek defines [38] *price value* as a cognitive compromise between the perceived benefits of the implemented solution and monetary costs. Users are more willing to adopt new technology when they perceive a positive price value and when the cost of using the technology is less significant than the benefits. The next three constructs are taken from the social area. We distinguish between other-orientation, which is an internal and pro-social motive, and self-care, which is an external motive. *Self-concern* orientation focuses on citizens taking specific actions aimed at achieving personal benefits [32]. F. Wijnhoven indicates [39] that caring for others (*other-orientation*) can be a motivating element to take action and increase commitment. This orientation is focused on the needs and interests of others, emphasizing the importance of caring for the weak and poor [32]. The final factor is citizens' willingness to belong to a group. The target group for crowdsourcing tools may be residents of a given housing estate or those living in a given geographical area. *Group oriented* membership may directly influence concern for others [40]. Therefore, it may be an element leading to the motivation and involvement of residents in crowdsourcing in the smart city area.

During the research, the author verified the following elements of the model that were achieved [29]: reliability of indicators in the model by examining external loadings, internal consistency using Cronbach's alpha, composite reliability and reliability coefficient, convergent validity through AVE analysis and discriminant validity using the Fornell-Lacker criterion, research cross-loadings and HTMT analysis. Then, the assessment of the structural model was analyzed by analyzing the VIF collinearity, the significance and accuracy of the structural model relationships by analyzing the path coefficients and significance levels of the given constructs along with the total effects for indirect relationships, and the bootstrapping method was used (estimating the distribution of estimation errors using multiple sampling with replacement from the sample). The explanatory power of R^2 for the models' endogenous variables, the f^2 coefficient, and the predictive power of Q^2 predictive validity were also analyzed.

A step in evaluating a structural model is to assess the significance and accuracy of the relationships that exist within the model. For this purpose, the analysis of path coefficients is used, i.e., estimated relationships of the structural model, which represent hypothetical relationships between the constructs included in the model. The strength of the association (path coefficient) represents the response of the dependent variable to a unit change in the explanatory variable when other variables in the model are held constant [41]. The path coefficients of a structural equation model (β) are similar to correlation or regression coefficients and are interpreted as follows:

1 A positive coefficient means that a unit increase in the activity measure of one structure leads to a direct increase in the activity measure of the structures onto which it projects, in proportion to the magnitude of the coefficient.
2 A negative coefficient means that an increase in the measure of activity in one structure leads to a direct, proportional decrease in the measure of activity of the structures onto which it projects (Fig. 1).

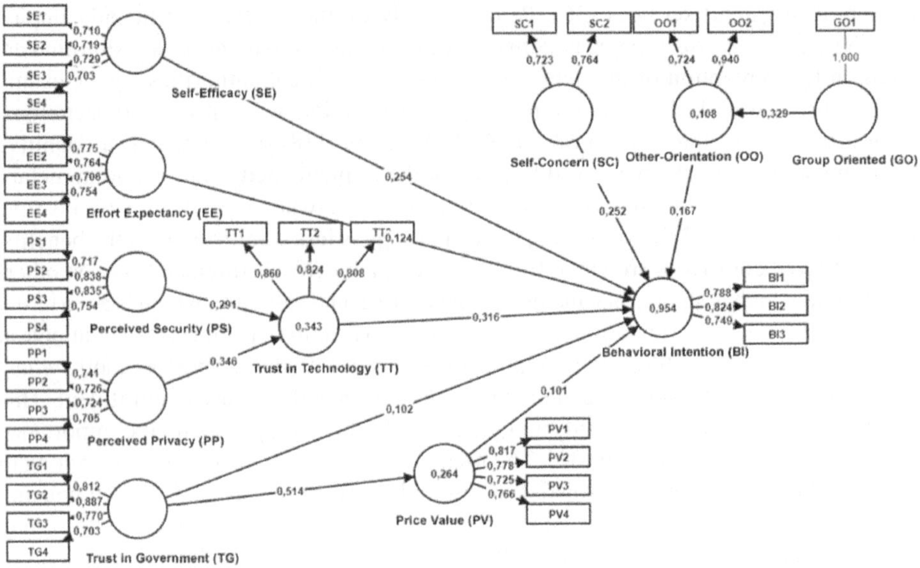

Fig. 1. Estimated structural indicators and external loadings for the Wroclaw (Poland) data sample.

Analyzing the values from the graph obtained from the survey conducted in Poland, it can be seen that the greatest influence on *behavioral intention* (BI), i.e. the willingness to participate in crowdsourcing, is *trust in technology* (TT) with a path coefficient of β = 0.316 (p = 0, is statistically significant), *self-efficacy* (SE) with the value β = 0.254 (p = 0, it is statistically significant), *self-concern* (SC) β = 0.252 (p = 0, it is statistically significant), *other orientation* β = 0.167 (p = 0.001, is statistically significant) and expected effort β = 0.124 (p = 0.041, is statistically significant). It can be assumed that the variables *trust in government* (TG) and *price value* (PV) have a weak impact on residents in terms of motivation to participate in crowdsourcing. Attention should also be paid to the strong relationship between *trust in government* (TG) variable and the *price value* (PV) variable, where the path coefficient is β = 0.514 (p = 0, it is statistically significant). The variables perceived privacy (PP) and *perceived security* (PS) have a large impact on *trust in technology* (TT), the values are β = 0.346 (p = 0, it is statistically significant) and β = 0.291, respectively.

(p = 0.003, is statistically significant). The influence is also visible in the case of the variable *group oriented* (GO) on the variable caring for others (OO), the path coefficient is β = 0.329 (p = 0, it is statistically significant).

A validation model based on data from Montpellier (France) showed similar conclusions.

5 Summary

Knowledge management and communication between decision-makers, stakeholders and residents are extremely important elements for the proper operation of each urban unit. The idea of a smart city provides for the possibility of implementing processes supporting the exchange of knowledge in cities, focusing on crowdsourcing activities. An example of a project that fits into urban crowdsourcing is a participatory budget.

The built crowdsourcing model is based on 11 constructs developed on the basis of literature, the UTAUT2 model and our own research. In both models, the author showed that the factors that influence residents' willingness to share knowledge and their involvement in crowdsourcing projects in the smart city area are: to the greatest extent *trust in technology* and *self-concern*, to a medium extent - sense of *self-efficacy*, *expected effort*, concern for others (*other orientation*), to a small extent - *trust in government* (local administration) and *price value*. Additionally, he observed a large impact of *perceived security* and *perceived privacy* on *trust in technology*, an impact of *trust in government* on *price value*, and a medium impact of focusing on the group (*group oriented*) on concern for others (*other orientation*).

References

1. U. N. Organization, World Urbanization Prospects, vol. 12. 2018
2. Duan, W., Nasiri, R., Karamizadeh, S.: Smart city concepts and dimensions. In: ACM International Conference Proceeding Series, pp. 488–492 (2019). https://doi.org/10.1145/3377170.3377189
3. Ghezzi, A., Gabelloni, D., Martini, A., Natalicchio, A.: Crowdsourcing: a review and suggestions for future research. Int. J. Manag. Rev. **20**(2), 343–363 (2018). https://doi.org/10.1111/ijmr.12135
4. Aziz, H., Shah, N.: Participatory budgeting: models and approaches. Comput. Sci. Game Theory, 215–236 (2021). https://doi.org/10.1007/978-3-030-54936-7_10
5. Komninos, N.: The age of intelligent cities: smart environments and innovation-for-all strategies (2014). https://doi.org/10.4324/9781315769349
6. Giffinger, R.: Smart cities ranking of European medium-sized cities. Res. Inst. Housing Urban Mobil. Serv., **16**, 1–24 (2007)
7. Lombardi, P., Giordano, S., Farouh, H., Yousef, W.: Modelling the smart city performance. Innov. Eur. J. Soc. Sci. Res. **25**(2), 137–149 (2012). https://doi.org/10.1080/13511610.2012.660325
8. Rudewicz, J.: Przemysł i technologie wobec wdrożenia wizji miasta inteligentnego (smart city). Stud. Ind. Geogr. Comm. Polish Geogr. Soc. **33**, 4 (2019). https://doi.org/10.24917/20801653.334.12
9. Rudewicz, J.: Model ekonomii współpracy w koncepcji miast smart. Przedsiębiorczość - Eduk. **15**(2), 152–170 (2019). https://doi.org/10.24917/20833296.152.11
10. Makieła, Z.J., Stuss, M.M., Mucha-Kuś, K., Kinelski, G., Budziński, M., Michałek, J.: Smart City 4.0: sustainable urban development in the metropolis GZM. Sustainable **14**, 6 (2022). https://doi.org/10.3390/su14063516
11. Sulich, A.: The green economy development factors. In: Vision 2020: Sustainable Economic Development and Application of Innovation Management from Regional expansion to Global Growth, pp. 6861–6869 (2018)

12. Yun, Y., Lee, M.: Smart City 4.0 from the perspective of open innovation. J. Open Innov. Technol. Mark. Complex. **5**, 4 (2019). https://doi.org/10.3390/joitmc5040092
13. Albino, V., Berardi, U., Dangelico, R.M.: Smart cities: definitions, dimensions, performance, and initiatives. J. Urban Technol. **22**(1), 3–21 (2015). https://doi.org/10.1080/10630732.2014.942092
14. Dirks, S., Keeling, M.: A Vision of Smarter Cities. New York IBM Global Services, p. 18 (2009)
15. Rohe, R., Rutkowska, M., Sulich, A.: Smart cities and challenges for European integration. In: International Conference European Integration, pp. 1240–1246 (2018)
16. Mercier-Laurent, E.: Greening and Smarting IT – Case of Digital Transformation, pp. 1–18 (2022). https://doi.org/10.1007/978-3-030-96592-1_1
17. Howe, J., Robinson, M.: The Rise of Crowdsourcing (2006). https://www.wired.com/2006/06/crowds/
18. Howe, J.: Crowdsourcing: A Definition (2006). https://crowdsourcing.typepad.com/cs/2006/06/crowdsourcing_a.html
19. Przysucha, Ł.: Crowdsourcing as a tool supporting intra-city communication, vol. 614 (2021). https://doi.org/10.1007/978-3-030-80847-1_7
20. Przysucha, Ł.: The concept of crowdsourcing in knowledge management in smart cities, vol. 599 (2021). https://doi.org/10.1007/978-3-030-85001-2_2
21. Bhatti, S.S., Gao, X., Chen, G.: General framework, opportunities and challenges for crowdsourcing techniques: a Comprehensive survey. J. Syst. Softw. **167**, 110611 (2020). https://doi.org/10.1016/j.jss.2020.110611
22. Owoc, M., Weichbroth, P.: Dynamical aspects of knowledge evolution (2020)
23. Przysucha, Ł.: Crowdsourcing and sharing economic in the smart city concept. Influence of the idea on development and urban resources, vol. 637 IFIP (2022). https://doi.org/10.1007/978-3-030-96592-1_2
24. Pondel, J., Pondel, M.: Enterprise communication tools supporting knowledge management processes. In: Proceedings 5th Artificial Intelligence for Knowledge Management (2017)
25. Vrabie, C., Tirziu, A.-M.: E-participation – a Key Factor in Developing Smart Cities. In: European Integration – Realities and Perspectives (EIRP), pp. 123–128 (2016)
26. Rytel-Warzocha, A.: Budżet obywatelski jako nowa forma społecznej partycypacji. Disputatio **1**, 65–77 (2013)
27. Radziszewski, M.: Budżet obywatelski instrumentem rozwoju kapitału społecznego. Athenaeum Pol. Stud. Politol. **51**(3), 131–154 (2016). https://doi.org/10.15804/athena.2016.51.08
28. Mohamad, M., Awang, Z.: Building corporate image and securing student loyalty in the Malaysian higher learning industry. J. Int. Stud. **4**(1), 30–40 (2009)
29. Hair, J., Hult, T., Ringle, C., Sarstedt, M.: A Primer on Partial Least Squares Structural Equation Modeling (PLS-SEM) (2021)
30. Venkatesh, V., Morris, M.G., Davis, G.B., Davis, F.D.: User acceptance of information technology: toward a unified view. MIS Q. Manag. Inf. Syst. **27**(3), 425–478 (2003). https://doi.org/10.2307/30036540
31. Habib, A., Alsmadi, D., Prybutok, V.R.: Factors that determine residents' acceptance of smart city technologies. Behav. Inf. Technol. **39**(6), 610–623 (2020). https://doi.org/10.1080/0144929X.2019.1693629
32. Abu-Tayeh, G., Neumann, O., Stuermer, M.: Exploring the motives of citizen reporting engagement: self-concern and other-orientation. Bus. Inf. Syst. Eng. **60**(3), 215–226 (2018). https://doi.org/10.1007/s12599-018-0530-8
33. Ajzen, I.: Perceived behavioral control, self-efficacy, locus of control, and the theory of planned behavior. J. Appl. Soc. Psychol. **32**(4), 665–683 (2002). https://doi.org/10.1111/j.1559-1816.2002.tb00236.x

34. Flammer, A.: Self-Efficacy. Self-Efficacy, Int. Encycl. Soc. Behav. Sci. Second Ed, pp. 504–508 (2015). https://doi.org/10.1016/B978-0-08-097086-8.25033-2
35. Tahar, A., Riyadh, H.A., Sofyani, H., Purnomo, W.E.: Perceived ease of use, perceived usefulness, perceived security and intention to use e-filing: the role of technology readiness. J. Asian Financ. Econ. Bus. **7**(9), 537–547 (2020). https://doi.org/10.13106/JAFEB.2020.VOL7.NO9.537
36. Nikkhah, H.R., Balapour, A., Sabherwal, R.: Mobile applications security: role of privacy. In: 24th Americas Conference on Information Systems 2018 Digit. Disruption, AMCIS 2018 (2018)
37. Kim, D.J., Ferrin, D.L., Rao, H.R.: A trust-based consumer decision-making model in electronic commerce: the role of trust, perceived risk, and their antecedents. Decis. Support. Syst. **44**(2), 544–564 (2008). https://doi.org/10.1016/j.dss.2007.07.001
38. Peek, S.T.M., Wouters, E.J.M., van Hoof, J., Luijkx, K.G., Boeije, H.R., Vrijhoef, H.J.M.: Factors influencing acceptance of technology for aging in place: a systematic review. Int. J. Med. Inform. **83**(4), 235–248 (2014). https://doi.org/10.1016/j.ijmedinf.2014.01.004
39. Wijnhoven, F., Ehrenhard, M., Kuhn, J.: Open government objectives and participation motivations. Gov. Inf. Q. **32**(1), 30–42 (2015). https://doi.org/10.1016/j.giq.2014.10.002
40. De Cremer, D., Leonardelli, G.J.: Cooperation in social dilemmas and the need to belong: the moderating effect of group size. Gr. Dyn. **7**(2), 168–174 (2003). https://doi.org/10.1037/1089-2699.7.2.168
41. Bollen, K.A.: Structural Equations with Latent Variables. Hoboken, NJ, USA: John Wiley & Sons, Inc. (1989). https://doi.org/10.1002/9781118619179

Utterance Analysis of Discussions Structure and Discourse Quality: A Case of Removed Soils in Fukushima Prefecture, Japan

Qinglin Cui[1], Yukihide Shibata[1], Tomohiro Hara[1], Yume Souma[1], Mie Tsujimoto[1], Takayuki Ito[2], and Susumu Ohnuma[1(✉)]

[1] Hokkaido University, N10 W7, Kita-Ku, Sapporo 060-0810, Japan
{sai,y-shibata,ohnuma}@let.hokudai.ac.jp, {hara.tomohiro.n7, souma.yume.16,tujimoto.mie.d0}@elms.hokudai.ac.jp

[2] Kyoto University, Yoshida-Honmachi, Kyoto 606-8501, Japan
ito@i.kyoto-u.ac.jp

Abstract. In this paper, we propose a multi-perspective analysis approach for discussion, integrating assessments of discussion structure and quality. As a demonstration experiment, we conducted an online discussion (OD) on the issue of removed soils in Fukushima Prefecture and gathered discussion data at Tokyo and Osaka. To compare the discussions in Tokyo and Osaka, the analysis was conducted using two methods: 1) Discussion structure analysis (IBIS), 2) discussion quality index (DQI). The IBIS results revealed a higher frequency of discussions on 'issues' in OD-Osaka compared to OD-Tokyo, while discussions on problem-solving 'ideas' were more prevalent in OD-Tokyo. In the DQI results, both OD-Tokyo and OD-Osaka consistently prioritized 'risk and cost', with less emphasis on 'burden sharing' and 'prioritizing the residents of Fukushima'. Comparing the two sets of results, OD-Tokyo exhibited a higher frequency of 'prioritizing risks and costs' and 'burden sharing', whereas OD-Osaka showed a higher frequency of 'prioritizing the residents of Fukushima'. Differences in discussion structure and quality among residents from different regions were evident through IBIS and DQI. The primary outcome revealed successful visualization of discussion data characteristics that couldn't be captured by a single evaluation scale.

Keywords: Utterance analysis · Discussion Data · Issue-Based Information System · Discourse Quality Index

1 Introduction

This research aims to depict the structure of public communication by analyzing discussion data with plural methodologies. To this end, we organized an online discussion (OD) on the issue of removed soils in Fukushima Prefecture, Japan. Subsequently, we will provide an overview of the OD implementation and present the findings.

Online cloud-scale discussion support systems have garnered attention as a next-generation democratic platform [1]. Studies have been conducted to evaluate the structural dynamics of discussions, introducing the Issue-Based Information System (IBIS)

W. Yin et al. (Eds.): IJCAI 2024, LNAI 14917, pp. 86–92, 2025.
https://doi.org/10.1007/978-981-97-9536-9_7

[2, 3], and assessing the quality of discourse through the Discourse Quality Index (DQI) [4–6]. Furthermore, a large-scale consensus support system has been implemented, integrating natural language processing and agent technology, with several social experiments validating its utility [7–9]. Thus, research in artificial intelligence-driven discussion support technology continues to advance steadily. From the perspective of human society, we have reached a critical juncture where the introduction and utilization of large-scale consensus support systems must be carefully analyzed.

However, there are dimensions of discussion evaluation that cannot be adequately captured through a singular evaluation metric. While the quality of a discussion hinges upon its content, it necessitates assessment from multiple vantage points, encompassing both the structural framework and the quality of utterances. Therefore, this paper presents an illustrative case of analyzing online discussions (ODs) through an amalgamation of methodologies to dissect the utterances' structure and quality. The discourse data derived from ODs facilitated by a Large-Scale Consensus Support System (D-Agree) undergoes two analytical modalities: Structural analysis utilizing IBIS and Discourse quality assessment via the DQI. Combining these two evaluation methods will give a high-relief view of the discourse over consensus and deliberation.

Given the growing interest in cloud-scale discussion support as a next-generation democracy platform, this paper aims to gather empirical evidence through analysis of discussion data.

2 Conducting Online Discussions

We conducted an online discussion on the issue of removed soils in Fukushima Prefecture as a demonstration experiment. This issue involves the final disposal of decontaminated soil outside Fukushima Prefecture.

We used the general-purpose service D-Agree as a large-scale consensus support system [9, 10]. D-Agree has a bulletin board for each theme, and participants enter free text and discuss each theme. Additionally, D-Agree employs an IBIS structure that allows for the evaluation of the discussion structure. The implemented automatic facilitation agent extracts the discussion structure from the text by automatically analyzing the IBIS structure, and proceeds with facilitation based on the extracted structure.

The discussion space provided by D-Agree was used to construct the OD implementation environment. We constructed two OD groups: OD-Tokyo and OD-Osaka (Fig. 1). The general citizens resided in the suburbs of Tokyo and Osaka and participated in workshops focused on the issue of the removed soils before the OD. We enrolled 23 participants in OD-Tokyo and 25 in OD-Osaka (ranging in age from their 20s to their 70s, with approximately equal numbers of men and women).

To avoid direct intervention in the conduct of the OD, the organizers solely provided reference materials, including 1) the D-Agree operating manual, 2) a concise explanation of the purpose (approximately 400 characters in Japanese), 3) presentation slides for preliminary information sharing (52 pages in PowerPoint format), 4) a summary of workshop discussion content (covering positive aspects, areas for improvement, and points of confusion), and 5) information provided by the Ministry of the Environment (via URL).

Participants could participate in OD at any time during the period by logging into the discussion space. The discussion period was two weeks, starting September 25th at OD-Tokyo and October 1st at OD-Osaka. Furthermore, participation in OD was not limited to the group in which the participant was registered. In addition, a one-week post-online discussion period was set up after the OD so that participants could review the content of the discussion. In this OD implementation, we always maintained a system of three people (three in charge, one leader) for preparation, such as participant registration, participant response (inquiries), and troubleshooting.

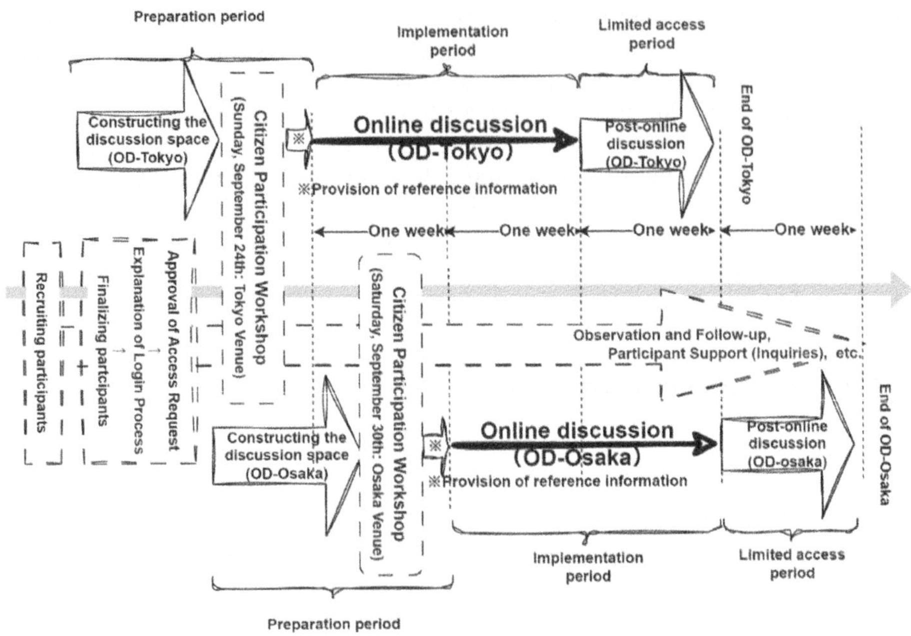

Fig. 1. Online discussions implementation flow diagram.

3 Analysis of Discussion Data

For our analysis, we employed the discussion datasets from OD-Tokyo and OD-Osaka. This section presents an overview of the datasets, outlines the analysis methodology, and presents the findings of the analysis for utterances and ODs.

3.1 Discussion Data and Analysis Methods

a) Discussion data

The text data from OD, comprising utterances from all participants, was obtained separately for OD-Tokyo and OD-Osaka from D-Agree. The discussion data encompasses 1) preparatory materials provided by the organizer, 2) inputs from the AI facilitator, and 3) utterances from all participants. This research exclusively focused on the utterances of participants in category 3). Table 1 presents the quantity of discussion data utilized in the analysis.

Table 1. Dataset overview.

Data set	Total number of utterances	Number of utterances used in analysis
OD-Tokyo	206	152
OD-Osaka	208	150

b) Used Analysis methods

The methods for evaluating the content of the discussion, the structure of the discussion, and the quality of the discussion were selected as shown in Table 2.

Table 2. Used Analysis methods.

Subject of evaluation	Analysis methods	Evaluation granularity
Discussion structure	IBIS	Sentence unit
discussion Quality	DQI	Utterance unit

To analyze the structure of discussions using IBIS, we utilized the analysis function implemented in D-Agree. Structural evaluation of discussions using the IBIS is a methodology that focuses on issues in the discussion, draws out ideas for solving the issues, and opinions on ideas in a hierarchical manner. Therefore, using IBIS results is useful in developing realistic and creative discussions [2, 3]. IBIS results are evaluated on a sentence-by-sentence basis, and to ensure consistency with other evaluation methods, we re-counted the sentence evaluation results based on utterances. When one utterance consists of multiple sentences, if any sentence has a corresponding code, the code for that utterance is also considered to be corresponding. Furthermore, our analysis employed the structural analysis feature of IBIS integrated within D-Agree [10]. The evaluation outcomes of IBIS were retrieved from D-Agree [10].

To analyze discussion quality, a revised version of the DQI [6] was employed, tailored to accommodate discussions involving the general public in Japan. Two independent coders, who were not involved in the discussions, performed the coding for the datasets.

Following a pre-provided manual, they independently assessed three items related to the common good: “prioritizing risk and cost,” “prioritizing burden sharing,” and “prioritizing the residents of Fukushima.“ To assess inter-rater reliability, the simple kappa coefficient was calculated, yielding $\kappa = .67$ for OD-Tokyo and $\kappa = .59$ for OD-Osaka. This analysis centered on the elements pertinent to the common good within the framework of the DQI. If an element pertained to the common good, it was assigned a score of 1. The percentage (%) was computed by taking the total count of instances where a score of 1 was attributed to each item about the common good as the denominator, and the count of instances where a score of 1 was assigned to each item as the numerator. However, considering discrepancies in evaluation outcomes among coders, instances where only one coder assigned a score of 1 were deemed as 0.5.

3.2 Analysis Results of Discussion Data and ODs

We present the analysis outcomes of the discussion data employing the chosen two methods, as depicted in Table 3. These findings are delineated separately for OD-Tokyo and OD-Osaka, categorized by method in matrix format. Leveraging these results, we are poised to conduct analyses of discussion data, combining different methods and delving into the content, structure, and quality of the discussions.

In the results of IBIS, the extracted data were aggregated into four categories: ’Issue’, ’Idea’, ’Merit’, and ’Demerit’. The numbers of ’merit’ and ’demerit’ opinions related to the idea were similar in both instances. However, the number of ’issues’ discussed was higher in OD-Osaka compared to OD-Tokyo. Conversely, the number of ’ideas’, proposed solutions to problems, was higher in OD-Tokyo than in OD-Osaka.

The results of DQI indicated a consistent inclination towards ’prioritizing risk and cost’ in both instances. A smaller number of utterances also included ’prioritizing burden sharing’ and ’prioritizing the residents of Fukushima.’ Upon comparison of the two sets of results, OD-Tokyo exhibited a relatively higher frequency of ’burden sharing’ than OD-Osaka. Conversely, OD-Osaka exhibited a higher frequency of ‘prioritizing the residents of Fukushima’ than OD-Tokyo.

4 Discussion and Summary

We organized ODs focusing on the issue of removed soils in Fukushima Prefecture, Japan. We successfully conducted a two-week ODs with approximately 20 participants by implementing a large-scale consensus support system. Given the number of participants, the findings from this study have limited explanatory power for large-scale discussions. However, considering the need for a forum where all participants can actively engage in the discussion, this reflects a relatively realistic scale of participation.

We utilized IBIS to analyze the discussion structure and DQI to evaluate discussion quality. The IBIS analysis revealed that opinions on "Idea" were more frequently categorized as "Demerit" rather than "Merit," suggesting that participants in this online discussion held relatively negative views and sentiments. The DQI results indicated that the focus remained "prioritizing risk and cost." Together, these results highlight the need

Table 3. ODs Analysis Results.

Methods	Category code	Results	
		OD-Tokyo	OD-Osaka
IBIS	Issue	0.6	8.4
	Idea	47.5	39.5
	Merit	22.4	21.0
	Demerit	29.5	31.1
DQI	Prioritizing risk and cost	77.1	80.0
	Prioritizing burden sharing	14.3	5.7
	Prioritizing the residents of Fukushima	8.6	14.3

※Percentage of extraction results by each method

for more inclusive discussions on other aspects of the "common good." Thus, the analysis provides new insights into the commonalities of online discussions (ODs) regarding the direction of discussions on the removed soils in Fukushima Prefecture.

We then quantified the differences in structure and quality between OD-Tokyo and OD-Osaka based on the results of the analysis. Given the similar conditions of both ODs, these findings likely reflect the inherent characteristics of the discussions in each location. Our methodology provided a more nuanced understanding of the discussions between OD-Tokyo and OD-Osaka, offering a two-dimensional perspective compared to traditional approaches. However, it is essential to acknowledge that this analysis focuses solely on comparing OD-Tokyo and OD-Osaka. Further validation studies are needed to generalize the evaluation of effective discussions.

By multi-perspective analyses employing different angles, it is possible to develop discussion support systems that depart from conventional approaches. Previous research [2–9] has shown that different analysis methods have unique focuses. An advantage of multi-perspective analysis is its capability to apply various viewpoints to a single discussion. As a result, discussions can be evaluated and supported based on factors like the topic, process, and flow of discourse. Looking ahead, such as IBIS, there is potential for the expansion of discussion support services by integrating diverse analytical functions into large-scale consensus support systems, facilitating real-time analysis.

We conducted an online discussion on the issue of removed soils in Fukushima Prefecture, Japan. Through the analyses of the discussions, we gained a more nuanced understanding of the dynamics within OD-Tokyo and OD-Osaka. It allowed us to concretely grasp the key points, flow, and progression of the discussions. While our research was limited to a comparative analysis of two ODs, accumulating practical examples of public discourse in the future holds promise for contributing to more generalized research outcomes and supporting discussions. In particular, comparing with instances of successful discourse evaluation can lead to the development of more specific and comprehensive support techniques. However, it's crucial to consider the impact of thematic variations when analyzing discussion cases. Especially in the context of support technologies utilizing natural language processing and supervised learning models, careful consideration is needed in the collection and organization of training data to ensure coverage across different themes or subdivisions of the topic.

Acknowledgment. This research received support from JST CREST (JPMJCR20D1), Grants-in-Aid for Scientific Research (22H01072, 23K04298), and the Environmental Research Promotion Fund (JPMEERF22S20906, JPMEERF22S20907). We employed D-Agree by Agreebitt Inc. as a large-scale consensus support system.

References

1. Malone, T.W.: Superminds: The Surprising Power of People and Computers Thinking Together, Little, Brown and Company (2018)
2. Kunz, W., Rittel, H.W.: Issues as elements of information systems, Technical report (1970)
3. Conklin, J., Begeman, M.L.: GIBIS: a tool for all reasons. J. Am. Soc. Inf. Sci. **40**(3), 200–213 (1989)
4. Steenbergen, MarcoR., B¨achtiger, A., Sp¨orndli, M., Steiner, J.: Measuring Political Deliberation—a Discourse Quality Index. In: Comparative European Politics, vol.1, no.1, pp. 21–48 (2003)
5. Fournier-Tombs, E., Di Marzo Serugendo, G.: Delib Analysis: understanding the quality of online political discourse with machine learning. J. Inf. Sci., 1–13 (2019)
6. Souma, Y., Yokoyama, M., Nakazawa, T., Tatsumi, T., Ohnuma, S.: The group discussion experiment on the treatment of removed low concentration soil outside fukushima prefecture: contemplation of common goods and the development of the index visualizing the discourse qualities. Jpn. J. Risk Anal. **32**(1), 11–23 (2022)
7. Ito, T., Fujita, K., Matsuo, T., Fukuta, N.: Innovating large-scale consensus support system based on agent technologies. J. Jpn. Soc. Artif. Intell. **32**(5), 739–746 (2017)
8. Imi, Y., Ito, T., Ito, T., Hideshima, E.: A development of consensus support system COLLAGREE and a pilot study towards internet-based town meeting in Nagoya. In: The 28th Annual Conference of the Japanese Society for Artificial Intelligence (2014)
9. Ito, T., et al.: Innovation of large-scale consensus support system based on agent technologies: a large-scale social experiment using the automated facilitation agent. In: The 33rd Annual Conference of the Japanese Society for Artificial Intelligence (2019)
10. AGREEBIT Inc. https://d-agree.com/site/

Obvious Independence of Clones
Extended Abstract

Ratip Emin Berker[1(✉)], Sílvia Casacuberta Puig[2], Isaac Robinson[2], and Christopher Ong[3]

[1] Foundations of Cooperative AI Lab (FOCAL), Carnegie Mellon University, Pittsburgh, PA 15213, USA
rberker@cs.cmu.edu
[2] University of Oxford, Oxford, UK
[3] Harvard University, Cambridge, MA 02138, USA

Abstract. The Independence of Clones (IoC) criterion measures a voting rule's robustness to strategic nomination. Prior literature has established empirically that individuals may still submit costly, distortionary misreports even in strategy-proof (SP) settings, due to failure to recognize the SP property. The intersection of these issues motivates the search for mechanisms that are *Obviously Independent of Clones (OIoC)*: where strategic nomination/exiting of clones obviously has no effect on the outcome. We construct a formal and intuitive definition of a voting rule being OIoC and examine five IoC rules to identify whether they satisfy OIoC.

1 Introduction

How can we prevent similar candidates in an election splitting the vote, leading to a less desirable winner? One answer is to require the voting rule to satisfy the *Independence of Clones (IoC)* criterion, which ensures that the addition or removal of a candidate with similar policy inclinations to others will not spoil the election [12]. While IoC rules have been well-studied in the computational social choice literature [3,5,10,12,14], it is not clear that the average voter or candidate can be easily convinced that any such rule is in fact IoC, resulting, for example, in a candidate unnecessarily dropping out of the race, either out of fear of hurting their party, or of being blamed by their voters for doing so.

As the benefits of a property are sometimes only accrued when agents believe it is satisfied, we turn to examining the *obviousness* of a property. Li [8] first defined *Obvious Strategy-Proof* mechanisms, which have since been studied in a variety of contexts [1,4,9,13]. As we will see, our notion of obviousness for IoC is inspired from the model of primary elections [7], which occurs within each political party (a practical approximation of a clone set) to decide on a joint candidate for a general election.

W. Yin et al. (Eds.): IJCAI 2024, LNAI 14917, pp. 93–97, 2025.
https://doi.org/10.1007/978-981-97-9536-9_8

2 Preliminaries

Model. Given a finite set of *voters* $N = [n]$ and *candidates* $A = \{a_i\}_{i\in[m]}$, each $i \in N$ has a strict *ranking* σ_i over A. A *preference profile* $\boldsymbol{\sigma}$ consists of all voters' rankings. A *voting rule* is a function that maps $\boldsymbol{\sigma}$ to a subset of A, the winner(s) of the election.

Definition 1 (Independence of Clones [12]). *A non-empty subset of candidates, $K \subseteq A$, is a* ***set of clones*** *with respect to $\boldsymbol{\sigma}$ if no voter ranks any candidate outside of K between any two elements of K. We say a voting rule is Independent of Clones (IoC) if:*

1. *A candidate that is a member of a set of clones wins if and only if some member of that set of clones wins after one of its clones is eliminated from the original ballot.*
2. *A candidate that is not a member of a set of clones wins if and only if that candidate wins after any clone is eliminated from the original ballot.*

Intuitively, a rule satisfying IoC ensures that the winner of an election does not change due to the addition of a candidate who is similar to an existing non-winning candidate.

Voting Rules Considered. We study five existing IoC rules, the definitions of which we provide in the full paper: *Single Transferable Vote (STV)*, *Ranked Pairs (RP)* [12], *the Schulze method* [11], *Schwartz rule* [2], and *Smith Alternative Vote (SAV)* [6].

3 Obvious Independence of Clones (OIoC) and Results

Before introducing the definition of OIoC, we first introduce two novel concepts:

Definition 2. *Given a preference profile $\boldsymbol{\sigma}$, a set of sets $\mathcal{K} = \{K_1, K_2, \ldots, K_\ell\}$ where $K_i \subseteq A$ for all $i \in [\ell]$ is a* ***clone partition with respect to $\boldsymbol{\sigma}$*** *if (1) $\mathcal{K}$ is a disjoint partitioning of A, and (2) each K_i is a non-empty clone set with respect to $\boldsymbol{\sigma}$.*

Definition 3 (GLOC). *Given any voting rule f,* ***GLOC$_f$*** *is a function that takes as input a preference profile $\boldsymbol{\sigma}$ and a clone partition $\mathcal{K}$ with respect to $\boldsymbol{\sigma}$ and performs:*
1. ***GLO****bal step: Given σ_i, say $\sigma_i^{\mathcal{K}}$ is the corresponding ranking over $\mathcal{K}$. Treating $\mathcal{K}$ as the set of candidates, compute $f\left(\boldsymbol{\sigma}^{\mathcal{K}}\right) \equiv f\left(\{\sigma_i^{\mathcal{K}}\}_{i\in N}\right)$ to get the 'winner clone sets'.*
2. ***LOC****al step: For each $K \in f\left(\boldsymbol{\sigma}^{\mathcal{K}}\right)$, say $\boldsymbol{\sigma}^K$ is $\boldsymbol{\sigma}$ with $A \setminus K$ removed. Compute $f(\boldsymbol{\sigma}^K)$ and output the union over all K such, i.e., $GLOC_f(\boldsymbol{\sigma}, \mathcal{K}) = \bigcup_{K\in f(\boldsymbol{\sigma}^{\mathcal{K}})} f(\boldsymbol{\sigma}^K)$*

Intuitively, GLOC first runs the input voting rule f on the clone sets (as specified by $\mathcal{K}$), 'packing' the candidates in each set to treat it as a candidate. It then 'unpacks' the clones within each winner clone set, and runs f once again among them. To demonstrate GLOC, we illustrate the protocol when applied to the setting of plurality voting f_{plur}, which simply picks the candidate who is the top choice for the most voters.

Vot.1	Vot.2	Vot.3	Vot.4	Vot.5	Vot.6	Vot.7
a	a	b	b	c	c	c
b	b	a	a	d	d	d
c	d	c	d	a	a	b
d	c	d	c	b	b	a

Fig. 1. An example preference profile $\boldsymbol{\sigma}$. Column Vot.i shows σ_i for Voter i

Consider $\boldsymbol{\sigma}$ from Fig. 1. We have $f_{plur}(\boldsymbol{\sigma}) = c$. Notice $\mathcal{K} = \{\{a, b\}, \{c, d\}\}$ is a valid clone partition with respect to $\boldsymbol{\sigma}$. Accordingly, GLOC maps $\{a, b\}$ and $\{c, d\}$ to the meta-candidates K_1 and K_2, respectively. As demonstrated in Fig. 2, we have $f_{plur}(\boldsymbol{\sigma}^{\mathcal{K}}) = K_1$. and $f_{plur}(\boldsymbol{\sigma}^{K_1}) = a$, implying $GLOC_{f_{plur}}(\boldsymbol{\sigma}, \mathcal{K}) = a$.

Vot.1	Vot.2	Vot.3	Vot.4	Vot.5	Vot.6	Vot.7
K_1	K_1	K_1	K_1	K_2	K_2	K_2
K_2	K_2	K_2	K_2	K_1	K_1	K_1

Vot.1	Vot.2	Vot.3	Vot.4	Vot.5	Vot.6	Vot.7
a	a	b	b	a	a	b
b	b	a	a	b	b	a

Fig. 2. (Left) $\boldsymbol{\sigma}^{\mathcal{K}}$, where the clone sets are condensed into singular candidates K_1 and K_2. (Right) $\boldsymbol{\sigma}^{K_1}$, where each σ_i is limited to the members of K_1

Having defined Clone Partitions and GLOC, we now formally introduce OIoC:

Definition 4. *A voting rule f is* ***Obviously Independent of Clones (OIoC)*** *if for all preference profile $\boldsymbol{\sigma}$ and all clone partitions $\mathcal{K}$ w.r.t. $\boldsymbol{\sigma}$, we have $f(\boldsymbol{\sigma}) = GLOC_f(\boldsymbol{\sigma}, \mathcal{K})$*

The example from Figs. 1 and 2 demonstrate that plurality is not OIoC, which is not surprising, considering the rule is not even IoC (as having a clone will split your plurality votes). In the full version of the paper, we formalize this hierarchy:

Proposition 1. *OIoC implies IoC.*

Most real-life elections do not result in ties. If we instead require agreement between f and $GLOC_f$ only when there is a clear winner, we get a natural relaxation of OIoC:

Definition 5. *A voting rule f is* ***weakly Obviously Independent of Clones (wOIoC)*** *if given any $\boldsymbol{\sigma}$ and any clone partition $\mathcal{K}$ w.r.t. $\boldsymbol{\sigma}$, $f(\boldsymbol{\sigma}) = \{a\}$ iff $GLOC_f(\boldsymbol{\sigma}, \mathcal{K}) = \{a\}$*

OIoC clearly implies wOIoC. The relationship between wOIoC and IoC is more nuanced: they are incomparable; however, (as discussed in the full version of the paper), wOIoC implies IoC under some reasonable assumptions about the voting rule. Having established the definitions of OIoC and wOIoC, we prove which rule satisfies which:

Theorem 1. *STV, the Schulze method, and SAV are not (even weakly) OIoC. Schwartz rule is wOIoC. Ranked pairs is OIoC.*

Of the five results, the most sophisticated is RP being OIoC. The proof depends on *impartial tie-breaking*, defined in [14], which is required for RP to always satisfy IoC.

4 Conclusion and Future Work

Definition 4 has a natural interpretation: if a voting rule is OIoC, then the outcome of the election will be same regardless of whether we (1) apply the rule directly or we (2) let the parties (clone sets) run primaries (pick their 'best' member) and run the election among these winners. Apart from this consistency result, it also has practical implications: if a rule is OIoC, the decision of a candidate to opt-out of an election can be postponed until after the winning parties are computed, hence removing any concern over a candidacy resulting in the loss of their party. Additionally, OIoC allows cutting expenses by eliminating primaries. Without primaries, OIoC rules can also derive clone sets a posteriori from the votes, rather than assuming a political party to be a clone set.

This paper opens several new lines of work. For instance, one could study the problem of extending other axioms from social choice (such as monotonicity or independence of irrelevant alternatives) to fit the framework of obviousness. More broadly, studying obviousness not only from a computational perspective but also an empirical or psychological point of view may shed light on how best to approach defining the obviousness of other axiomatic properties.

References

1. Ashlagi, I., Gonczarowski, Y.A.: Stable matching mechanisms are not obviously strategy-proof. J. Econ. Theory **177**, 405–425 (2018). https://doi.org/10.1016/j.jet.2018.07.001. http://dx.doi.org/10.1016/j.jet.2018.07.001
2. Deb, R.: On Schwartzs rule. J. Econ. Theory **16**(1), 103–110 (1977). https://doi.org/10.1016/0022-0531(77)90125-9. http://dx.doi.org/10.1016/0022-0531(77)90125-9
3. Elkind, E., Faliszewski, P., Slinko, A.: Clone structures in voters preferences. In: Proceedings of the 13th ACM Conference on Electronic Commerce, EC 2012. ACM, June 2012. https://doi.org/10.1145/2229012.2229050. https://doi.org/10.1145/2229012.2229050

4. Ferraioli, D., Ventre, C.: Obvious strategyproofness needs monitoring for good approximations. In: Proceedings of the AAAI Conference on Artificial Intelligence, vol. 31, no. 1, February 2017. https://doi.org/10.1609/aaai.v31i1.10588. http://dx.doi.org/10.1609/aaai.v31i1.10588
5. Freeman, R., Brill, M., Conitzer, V.: On the axiomatic characterization of runoff voting rules. In Proceedings of the AAAI Conference on Artificial Intelligence, vol. 28, no. 1, June 2014. https://doi.org/10.1609/aaai.v28i1.8827. http://dx.doi.org/10.1609/aaai.v28i1.8827
6. Green-Armytage, J.: Four condorcet-hare hybrid methods for single-winner elections. In: Voting Matters – To Advance the Understanding of Preferential Voting Systems, pp. 1–14 (2011)
7. Gurian, P.H., Burroughs, N., Atkeson, L.R., Cann, D., Haynes, A.A.: National party division and divisive state primaries in U.S. presidential elections, 1948-2012. Polit. Behav. **38**(3), 689–711 (2016). https://doi.org/10.1007/s11109-016-9332-1. http://dx.doi.org/10.1007/s11109-016-9332-1
8. Li, S.: Obviously strategy-proof mechanisms. Am. Econ. Rev. **107**(11), 3257–3287 (2017). https://doi.org/10.1257/aer.20160425. http://dx.doi.org/10.1257/aer.20160425
9. Li, S.: On the computational properties of obviously strategy-proof mechanisms. SSRN Electron. J. (2020). https://doi.org/10.2139/ssrn.3747819. http://dx.doi.org/10.2139/ssrn.3747819
10. Parkes, D., Xia, L.: A complexity-of-strategic-behavior comparison between Schulzes rule and ranked pairs. In: Proceedings of the AAAI Conference on Artificial Intelligence, vol. 26, no. 1, pp. 1429–1435 (2021). https://doi.org/10.1609/aaai.v26i1.8258. http://dx.doi.org/10.1609/aaai.v26i1.8258
11. Schulze, M.: A new monotonic, clone-independent, reversal symmetric, and condorcet-consistent single-winner election method. Soc. Choice Welfare **36**(2), 267–303 (2010). https://doi.org/10.1007/s00355-010-0475-4. http://dx.doi.org/10.1007/s00355-010-0475-4
12. Tideman, T.N.: Independence of clones as a criterion for voting rules. Soc. Choice Welfare **4**(3), 185–206 (1987). https://doi.org/10.1007/bf00433944. http://dx.doi.org/10.1007/bf00433944
13. Troyan, P.: Obviously strategyproof implementation of top trading cycles. Int. Econ. Rev. **60**(3), 1249–1261 (2019). https://doi.org/10.1111/iere.12384. http://dx.doi.org/10.1111/iere.12384
14. Zavist, T.M., Tideman, T.N.: Complete independence of clones in the ranked pairs rule. Soc. Choice Welfare **6**(2), 167–173 (1989). https://doi.org/10.1007/bf00303170. http://dx.doi.org/10.1007/bf00303170

Poster

A Platform for Finding the Truth in Multiple Questions Polls

Quentin Elsaesser[1], Patricia Everaere[2], Alain Kemgue[1], and Sébastien Konieczny[1](✉)

[1] CRIL, CNRS - Université d'Artois, 62300 Lens, France
elsaesser@cril.fr , kemgue@cril.fr , konieczny@cril.fr
[2] LIFL, CNRS - Université de Lille, 59650 Villeneuve d'Ascq, France
patricia.everaere-caillier@univ-lille.fr

Abstract. We propose a method to find the truth in settings when several agents provide claims about several questions. We show that this method outperforms methods from the literature. We also propose an online platform for making this method available for improved group-decision making and for obtaining more real-world benchmarks.

Keywords: Truth tracking · Wisdom of the Crowds · Platform for e-democracy

1 Introduction

Democratic decisions are known to be efficient for epistemic questions (i.e. questions for which there is a *correct* answer). This is the topic of Condorcet's Jury Theorem and its extensions [1–4, 6–8, 10, 11, 14]. But in all these works there is only one question to be answered.

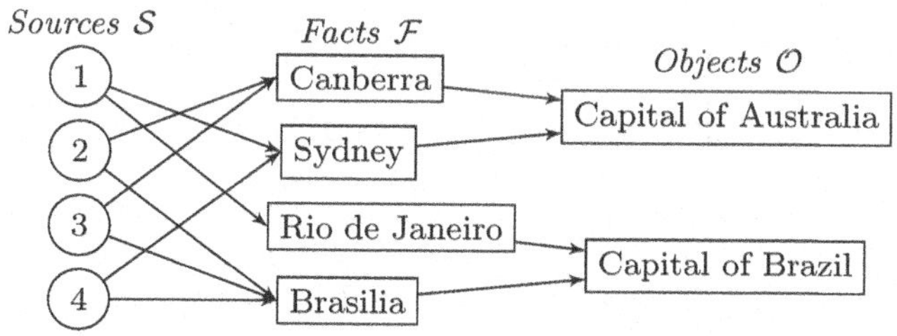

Fig. 1. Sources, Facts & Objects

We focus on a framework where there are several questions (called *Objects*), as in Fig. 1, and where the reliability of the individuals/sources is unknown and not uniform. We propose iterative methods in order to estimate the reliability of the individuals/sources, and to evaluate the credibility of the potential answers

W. Yin et al. (Eds.): IJCAI 2024, LNAI 14917, pp. 101–103, 2025.
https://doi.org/10.1007/978-981-97-9536-9

(called *Facts*) to these questions. And we show the effectiveness of our methods compared to pure majority and to methods from the literature for this truth-tracking tasks on experiments.

We have developped a platform, Truthicize.com, where people can create some polls, to get people's opinion, and use our methods to find the truth. This platform will also allow us to obtain more real-world benchmarks.

2 Source and Facts (S&F) Methods

We do not have enough space to detail our methods, but the reader can find them here [5]. Roughly, in the first iteration we assign the same reliability to all the sources, and then we compare the answers to the different questions. We reward the sources that answer like the majority, relying on the idea of Condorcet's Jury Theorem [11], which states that it is more likely that the majority of the individuals will choose the correct solution (this can also be seen as an application of the "wisdom of the crowds" [16]). To reward the sources, the objects take part to a vote where they rank their related facts from most reliable to least reliable ones. We use scoring-based voting rules in order to assign a number to each fact rank. The new reliability of each source is computed by combining all these scores. Then a new iteration starts with the updated reliability of each source. The algorithm stops when the process converges or after 30 iterations.

For instance, in Fig. 1, the majority claims that *Brasilia* is the *Capital of Brazil* but there is a tie for the *Capital of Australia*. The sources claiming *Brazilia* get a reward for proposing the most popular answer (which is then considered as the most plausible one). Then, in the next iteration, the credibility of *Camberra* will be better than the credibility of *Sydney*, and then sources 2, 3 and 4 will be considered more reliable than source 1, and we will choose *Camberra*.

We have shown on experiments that our methods outperform methods from the literature [9, 13, 15, 17] for the task of finding the correct answer (the truth) to the different questions on experiments on synthetic and real data. We have also shown that our methods can estimate the true reliability of the sources/individuals. The reader can find the results in [5].

3 A Platform for Finding the Truth

We have developed an online platform, Truthicize.com, where people can create some polls, get people's opinion, and use our methods to find the truth.

We hope that this platform will be useful to help people make better (i.e. more correct) decisions in multiple questions polls, and that it can be a useful tool for e-democracy.

The platform also allows to give figures and explanations on how the results are obtained. It can therefore be used for educational purposes, to highlight the effectiveness of democratic decisions on epistemic questions.

But this platform will also allow us to obtain more real benchmarks to further develop these truth-finding methods. We will make these (anonymised) benchmarks available to the community.

Acknowledgements. This work has benefited from the support of the AI Chair BE4musIA of the French National Research Agency (ANR-20-CHIA-0028).

References

1. Austen-Smith, D., Banks, J.: Information aggregation, rationality, and the Condorcet jury theorem. Am. Polit. Sci. Rev. **90**, 34–45 (1996)
2. Ben-Yashar, R., Paroush, J.: A nonasymptotic Condorcet jury theorem. Soc. Choice Welfare **17**(2), 189–199 (2000)
3. Ben-Yashar, R., Zahavi, M.: The Condorcet jury theorem and extension of the franchise with rationally ignorant voters. Public Choice **148**(3/4), 435–443 (2011)
4. Berend, D., Paroush, J.: When is Condorcet's jury theorem valid? Soc. Choice Welfare **15**(4), 481–488 (1998)
5. Elsaesser, Q., Everaere, P., Konieczny, S.: Voting-based methods for evaluating sources and facts reliability. In: 35th IEEE International Conference on Tools with Artificial Intelligence, ICTAI 2023, Atlanta, GA, USA, 6-8 November 2023, pp. 178–185. IEEE (2023)
6. Estlund, D.: Opinion leaders, independence, and Condorcet's jury theorem. Theor. Decis. **36**(2), 131–162 (1994)
7. Everaere, P., Konieczny, S., Marquis, P.: The epistemic view of belief merging: can we track the truth? In: Nineteenth European Conference on Artificial Intelligence (ECAI'10), pp. 621–626 (2010)
8. Hummel, P.: Jury theorems with multiple alternatives. Soc. Choice Welfare **34**(1), 65–103 (2010)
9. Kleinberg, J.M.: Authoritative sources in a hyperlinked environment. J. ACM (JACM) **46**(5), 604–632 (1999)
10. List, C., Goodin, R.E.: Epistemic democracy: generalizing the Condorcet jury theorem. J. Polit. Philos. **9**(3), 277–306 (2001)
11. Marquis de Condorcet: Essai sur l'application de l'analyse à la probabilité des décisions rendues à la pluralité des voix. Imprimerie royale Paris (1785)
12. Owen, G., Grofman, B., Feld, S.L.: Proving a distribution-free generalization of the Condorcet jury theorem. Math. Soc. Sci. **17**(1), 1–16 (1989)
13. Pasternack, J., Roth, D.: Knowing what to believe (when you already know something). In: Proceedings of the 23rd International Conference on Computational Linguistics (Coling 2010), pp. 877–885 (2010)
14. Peleg, B., Zamir, S.: Extending the Condorcet jury theorem to a general dependent jury. Soc. Choice Welfare **39**(1), 91–125 (2012)
15. Singleton, J., Booth, R.: Towards an axiomatic approach to truth discovery. J. Auton. Agent. Multi-Agent Syst. **36**(2), 1–49 (2022)
16. Surowiecki, J.: The Wisdom of Crowds: Why the Many are Smarter Than the Few and How Collective Wisdom Shapes Business, Economies. Doubleday, Societies and Nations (2004)
17. Yin, X., Han, J., Yu, P.S.: Truth discovery with multiple conflicting information providers on the web. IEEE Trans. Knowl. Data Eng. **20**(6), 796–808 (2008)

Author Index

W. Yin et al. (Eds.): IJCAI 2024, LNAI 14917, p. 105, 2025.
https://doi.org/10.1007/978-981-97-9536-9

The manufacturer's authorised representative in the EU is Springer Nature Customer Service Centre GmbH, Europaplatz 3, 69115 Heidelberg, Germany. If you have any concerns regarding our products, please contact ProductSafety@springernature.com

Printed and bound by CPI Group (UK) Ltd, Croydon, CR0 4YY
25/09/2026
02222647-0015